13 STRADOMSKA STREET

T0161530

13 STRADOMSKA STREET

A Memoir of Exile and Return

ANDREW POTOK

[M]

MANDEL VILAR PRESS

This book is typeset in Monotype Dante. The paper used in this book meets the minimum requirements of ANSI/NISO Z39.48-1992 (R1997). ∞

Designed by Barbara Werden

Library of Congress Cataloging-in-Publication Data
Names: Potok, Andrew, author.
Title: 13 Stradomska Street : a memoir of exile and return / Andrew Potok.
Other titles: Thirteen Stradomska Street : a memoir of exile and return
Description: Simsbury, Connecticut : Mandel Vilar Press, 2017.
    Identifiers: LCCN 2016046177 | ISBN 9781942134305 (paperback)
    Subjects: LCSH: Potok, Andrew—Travel—Poland. | Holocaust, Jewish (1939-1945)—Poland—Personal narratives. | Holocaust, Jewish (1939-1945)—Psychological aspects. | Blind painters—United States—Biography. | BISAC: BIOGRAPHY & AUTOBIOGRAPHY / Personal Memoirs. | HISTORY / Jewish. | SOCIAL SCIENCE / Jewish Studies. | HISTORY / Modern / 20th Century.
Classification: LCC ND237.P814 A2 2017 | DDC 759.9438—dc23
    LC record available at https://lccn.loc.gov/2016046177

Printed in the United States of America
16 17 18 19 20 21 22 23 24 / 9 8 7 6 5 4 3 2 1

Mandel Vilar Press
19 Oxford Court, Simsbury, Connecticut 06070
www.americasforconservation.org | www.mvpress.org

For Mark and For Sarah

PROLOGUE

During the war, German thugs turned my family's elegant showrooms on Marszalkowska, the Champs-Elysees of Warsaw, into a brothel. I had once played on those silver couches, reflected in the mirrors hung on every wall. I ran my little fingers along the Alaskan seals and Persian lambs, slid mink coats back and forth with my uncle on the long mahogany tables.

In the mid-1950s, based on the testimony of a witness who watched Goering and Himmler send trucks full of Apfelbaum fur coats from Warsaw to Berlin, my mother and my uncle received reparations money from the Germans. This witness, a former cutter in the Apfelbaum factory, now sat on a luxurious couch in the Maximilian Furs showroom on Fifty-Seventh Street in New York and told us astonishing wartime stories.

An SS Hauptsturmfuehrer named Fassbender marched into the fur salon and "Aryanized it." Fassbender began an affair with Slawa, one of Apfelbaum's beautiful models, and they moved into my parents' apartment at Moniuszki Four, possibly into my blue bedroom and nursery. Slawa was half Russian, married to a Polish officer. She became Fassbender's accomplice as well as his lover. He impregnated her—in my bed?—and arranged for her husband to be arrested and shot by the Gestapo.

In the Germany of the 1950s, resistance to paying restitution to Jews was huge. According to several public opin-

VII

ion polls recorded after the war had ended, only five percent of West Germans felt guilty about the devastation they had inflicted, and only twenty-nine percent believed that Jews were owed restitution. The rest were divided between those who thought that only those Germans who committed inhuman crimes were responsible and should pay, and those who thought that the Jews themselves were partly responsible for what happened to them during the German occupation. Anyone who suggested a societal responsibility for the Holocaust was branded as a foolish victim of Jewish propaganda.

The German payment to Maximilian Furs helped my uncle Max buy top of the line sable pelts from Leningrad and Canada, helped redecorate their already-plush showrooms, and helped finance my graduate school and my years of painting in Paris.

Now, more than fifty years later, a Polish lawyer calls me in Vermont, urging me to claim an apartment house once owned by my grandmother. I was eight years old when, as we were about to flee, my grandmother Paulina held me in her arms on the pavement in front of our Warsaw apartment, a vague distant memory.

The Polish lawyer speaks decent English. "You must come," he says, "to claim a property which is rightfully yours." My heart is beating hard but I don't know if I can bear going back to revisit awful memories, traumas, hatreds, and betrayals.

PART ONE

1

SIGNS FROM ABOVE

1.

Among the five houses on my street are two signs put up by the city. One declares that we are a DEAD END STREET with no easy turnaround. A couple of houses down, another warns that there is NO PARKING on Richardson Street; it's not a drive-through, a heartwarming thought. The street ends abruptly one house up from ours in a cluster of trees and bushes that mark the border of Hubbard Park, which overlooks Montpelier, the tiny capital of Vermont.

Each year for the past few years, usually toward the end of May, a woodpecker selects the dead end sign instead of a tree intended for his delectation, inside whose trunk and limbs he would find a reward for his evolution-given skills, a worm or a bug.

The woodpecker's pitiful pecking on a steel sign touches my heartstrings. I am awash in anthropomorphic sympathy. But wherever the bird chooses to perform his nervous pecking, I do understand that it is his love song, his attempt at broadcasting his presence to lady woodpeckers in the hope of getting laid. Though the tapping reverberates like a jackhammer in my ears, I feel sorry for the damn bird, fool that

I am about animal pain or stupidity. When I read about a beached whale or hear a cat screeching in the middle of the night, it makes my body shake and shudder. But I could be out there perched on the dead end sign with the woodpecker, banging away at my love song, and it would do me about as much good as it does for this crazy bird. "That bird is sending you a message," says my wife, Loie, who is sitting on the porch chair opposite me.

"You're saying that this is a sign from above? He's talking to me?"

"You should pay some attention. He is definitely pointing out the dead end sign."

"Maybe you've spent too many years in California," I jab. She swats my knee. But ever since an old friend accosted me in front of the post office to say that he had found God in the roar of a nor'easter, I've become wary of nutcases reading signs. I reach across the little wicker table between us and take Loie's hand in mine. "Actually, looking into the dead ends of my life might be kind of interesting."

"See what I mean? That bird is telling you what your next book should be about," Loie says. "On the other hand," she adds, "Richardson Street is not really a dead end. Once you push your way through brambles and branches and roots, you're in another landscape. Not only that, but dead ends often lead to new ways of seeing things."

"The damn woods are a dead end for me," I grumble. My guide dog, Gabriel, might notice a branch hanging low, about to poke me in the eye, and then again he might not. Loie is all eyes. I'm all ears.

I follow her into the house. "I don't know if I have another book in me," I complain as Gabriel, off harness, follows us in. "Maybe I'm too damn old," I kvetch.

"You're not so old," she says.

"No?" I lift my chin a little to check for wattles. Vanity will follow me to my grave.

At the dining room table, I pour each of us a glass of red wine. Loie rearranges the white lilies she has brought in from the garden, then gets up to draw the curtains. "Your last book was worth it," she says. "You dealt with very important issues. You found a new way to look back at your father. You couldn't have gotten better therapy." Loie is a psychotherapist, and psychological considerations have taken on a new and not always welcome importance in my life.

"Jesus, Loie, it wasn't therapy. It was . . . a book."

"It wasn't therapy?" she asks, getting perturbed now. "Your own father was the bane of your existence and you transformed him in your book into a father you wanted and needed. That's not therapy?"

"Art is not therapy and art therapy is not art." I have never been clear about the art-life distinction, the need of biography in the understanding of art. My wife's interest is in relationships rather than the ineffability of the art object.

"Anyway," Loie says, dismissing my little retort, "all I'm saying is that you seem unhappy just sitting home and reading. What are you reading anyway?"

"About the war."

"That's what I mean. You always read depressing books." She reaches back to the credenza for her knitting.

"Philip Roth stopped writing and he's a year younger than me."

"Two years," she corrects.

"One and a half."

"He wrote more than thirty books," she taunts. "You wrote four."

I pour myself more wine. Now I'm really getting depressed. "The only thing I know how to write about is me. I'm sick of writing about me."

She puts her knitting down, gets up, and heads for the kitchen. "I have to start marinating the meat for tomorrow," she says. I follow her in. She leafs through her Italian cookbook. I lean against one of the new cabinets, open and close a drawer that's supposed to close itself. I walk away and a corner of the butcher-block island smacks my hip, making my jaws clench. The dentist calls my attention to this every time I see him. Yes, yes, I clench and grind and my bite is too strong. My rotting teeth are my fault, not yours. I punish the hard wood island with my fist. Loie doesn't notice. She is humming some singer-songwriter tune and, as she crashes her way through all the pots looking for the right one, she says, "Excuse me a minute. I'm going to make some noise," and she turns on the mixer.

I find the living room couch, lean my head back, and my brain begins to whir with poignant memories of grabbing at life, choosing from column A, then column B. I could have chosen anything: history, philosophy, art, music. A wife, then two, three, maybe more. I remember feeling full, every breath a gulp, screaming, crying, drunk with laughter. Not so much any more. But things aren't so bad. It has been a full life, already a long life, fifteen years more than my father's, five to go until ninety when my mother died; but thinking of death is not a good way to avoid depression, so I remember the exquisite feel of horse chestnuts in the Saski Gardens in Warsaw, blobs of cadmium red and ivory black on my palette, the sight of the giant black ships in the Baltic Sea, hearing the key of G minor for the first time, skipping down flights of stairs, my feet hardly touching, the sweet scent of roses in a Zopot garden where a little girl let me watch her pee. The smell of chicken wafts in from the kitchen and I take a long, satisfied breath, then travel back to the Spanish hills where I lie down under the spreading gnarled oaks, then look up at the marble mountains of Carrara, at the fishing boats in Greek island village harbors. I jump onto the moving Paris bus—Number Sixty-Eight?

Eighty-Seven?—from the rue de Passy to Saint-Germain-des-Pres.

"Where have you been?" Loie asks, squatting beside me. "You should get some fresh air."

I shake off nostalgia and saddle up the great Gabriel and, his harness on and tail wagging, we begin the descent of Richardson Street, hoping that movement and the last of this day's sunlight will get me back to the present. I allow Gabriel three pee stops on the way to town. When he is unable to squeeze out another drop, we pass the gate of the State House grounds, then sit on the lawn in front of the capitol building near the marigolds and geraniums. After sniffing around for evidence of his species, Gabriel lies down at my side.

When enough rods and cones of my retina were buried under a build-up of gunk, I stopped painting and began to write fiction and non-fiction: running for a cure for my blindness, non-fiction; a kid coming of age as an artist, sold as fiction, only partly non-fiction; a book of interviews with people working in various aspects of disability, strictly non-fiction; then a fiction-non-fiction mix in which I transformed my miserable father into a vigorous, loving one. What now? Advice to the aging? Tales of love and boredom? A compilation of life's dead ends? Many come to mind, foremost among them blindness, not to speak of life itself. For some of my friends, even death is not a dead end, but their way to heaven or reincarnation or some damn thing.

With Gabriel snoring gently now, I concentrate on my breath. "Breathe into it," I hear my friend Robert's voice. Into what? I keep wondering. So I begin breathing deeply, then exhale fully, "the Ujjayi breath" he calls it, but it isn't working. A private plane practices cutting its engine above me and I get goose bumps, having distrusted low-flying airplanes since childhood.

7

Back home, Gabriel goes straight to the downstairs toilet for a long drink of water, after which I take the harness off him.

At noon the next day, the telephone rings. An unfamiliar voice on the other end, accented in a most familiar way. The man identifies himself as a Polish lawyer. He labors with his English. There is, he tells me, stuttering a little, a property in Poland, once my grandmother's and wrongly inherited by someone whose identity I don't quite catch.

"I am confident," he says, "that we will re-re-recover and sell this property which is rightfully yours."

I'm supposed to believe this?

"I p-p-propose to bring you and your wife, at my expense, to Krakow," the voice continues. "You must testify in a Polish court." He pauses. "I pay for everything," he assures me, "the f-f-flight to Krakow, your hotel here, all your expenses."

"I don't understand," I say. "Tell me again. I'm to recover what and what is it worth?"

"It is a small apartment house and, I am sure, worth a substantial amount. It depends on the currency exchange at the time we settle this. It could be much more than two hundred thousand."

"Dollars?"

"D-d-dollars."

Loie and I are self-employed, she a psychotherapist, I, once a painter and now a writer, so no retirement pensions in our old age. The state of our finances has always been precarious. I lost quite a lot of invested money in the late 1980s because of very bad advice. Most of the remainder disappeared in a guilt-ridden divorce settlement in the late 1990s. The money from writing is sporadic. If the recovery money from this Polish lawyer's proposal were to come through, it would be a welcome relief. But who is this guy? Things like this don't happen except in Greek plays. Then I remember the phone calls when my third book was being considered for publication and the editor at Random House offered my agent a puny advance.

"Seven and a half thousand," my agent reported to me on the phone.

"After all these years of work," I said, feeling totally deflated, "let's ask for ten at the very least."

Later that day, my agent called and said, "Andy, you'd better sit down." I did, expecting the worst. "Seven and a half meant seventy-five and when I insisted on at least ten, they agreed to a hundred thousand dollar advance." Remembering this, an impossible turn of events that every writer must dream about, I wonder what the chances are of lightning striking twice.

The Polish lawyer has been talking all this time. "So what's in it for you?" I ask.

"In it?"

"I mean that surely you intend to make money from this."

"When it is f-f-finished," he says, "I will take thirty percent. But f-f-first we need many documents, power of attorney, contracts, your parents' death certificates, your birth certificate, many things."

"I don't have a birth certificate," I tell him and wonder what documents my parents brought with us, what they had time to collect, what documents were necessary to enter Lithuania, Latvia, Sweden, and the United States.

This doesn't seem to bother him. He says, "You s-s-simply have to show up for two court hearings where you will t-t-testify regarding the former existence and death of certain members of your f-f-family and establish the reason for your claim."

When Loie comes home after work, I am still sitting by the phone. "I can't believe it," Loie says. She is excited, undoubtedly already imagining the movie that will be made of the Polish experience in the same way she dreams of who will play whom every time some Hollywood producer becomes even vaguely interested in making a movie of one of my books. "Even if no money comes from all this," Loie says, "a dead end it won't be. You can always write about it." I swivel my chair to face her, lay my hands on her hips. "We'll have an adventure," she says.

When Loie was in her early twenties and I in my mid-thirties, she knocked on the door of my studio. In jeans and an untucked man's shirt, she was a lithe startling pony with a gap between her two front teeth. Even that costume couldn't hide her large breasts and hips. I was immersed in a big sloppy semi-abstract interior, afire with slashed and dripping reds and yellows.

"Am I disturbing you?" she asked, closing the door behind her. "I heard that there was an artist working a couple of houses down from where I'm staying." She looked like she should be dancing, not walking, as it happened, on bare feet. She came over and stood behind me. "Oh my," she said, "It's so full of life. Those colors," she went on, her hands now on her temples, "they're so . . . I don't know . . . passionate. They make my body tingle."

What could I do except lay down the brush, still heavy with pigment and pay full attention to this marvelous apparition? Life does not offer many such moments, such life-enhancing opportunities, a beautiful woman presenting herself and asking to know me. I wiped off a stool. "Please sit," I said, smiling, the courtly artist, the European gentleman.

Instead, she hoisted herself up onto a sturdy desktop strewn with tubes of paint. "My name is Loie," she said. "I'm volunteering up at the group home to help take care of a bunch of troubled boys." Her fingers were drumming on the bureau top, their sound and her loveliness enthralling. "I went to Pratt," she told me, "until a filthy professor refused to give me a passing grade unless I slept with him."

"They can still pull that shit?"

"So I quit," Loie said.

"You left art school? So now what?"

"I don't know," she said. "Maybe babies." I sat down on a stool facing her and bared my Slavic soul to her—both Slavic and Jewish, the perfect combination of gallantry and erudition. And what is the difference anyway between fiction and non-fiction as long as there's art in it? So I told her how, at times, I couldn't paint because I was so aroused, breathing hard, needing to splash cold water on my body. I told her that putting brush to canvas was, at times, a life and death situation. I told her of the darkness in my soul. And then we both confessed that we were married, each of us a short time ago, my second, her first. But the air remained heavy with desire, expectation. We looked directly into each other's eyes, hers large and beautiful. We each backed off a little, but only a little. A few weeks later, she and her husband left for California and I settled back down with my wife, Charlotte. Loie and I did not see or hear from each other for twenty-five years. She stayed on her coast and I stayed on mine.

2.

Now we drive to a walking path in Stowe. Gabriel is a good puller. We walk briskly, which I enjoy, but I realize that we should probably leave him at home for our week or so in Krakow. The last time I was in Poland, twenty-five years ago, Dash, my first Seeing Eye dog, traveled with us, a mistake partly because I had enough eyesight then to walk comfortably on my son's or Charlotte's arm, partly because we spent a lot of time driving in our hired taxi. Guide dogs were not a common sight, and though many Poles owned dogs, they were not allowed in hotels or restaurants, making for unpleasant squabbles wherever we went. When, after Poland, we flew with my son to Madrid where he and his wife were living, Dash jumped out of a car window on the road to Cuenca. Once he was settled back in and we had safely arrived in town, we left Dash in the car so we could cross the Puente de San Pablo, a very narrow bridge forty meters above a dramatic gorge. Pissed off, Dash destroyed the seats of Mark's Toyota. Some dogs are not great car travelers and Gabriel belongs to that tribe, not enraged like Dash but miserable in a car.

On the Stowe path, bicycles zoom past us, the nice Vermont riders yelling, "Coming on your left." We sit down on a bench near a running brook and let Gabriel stomp around in the water.

I've always loved the Sam Gross cartoon of the blind guy, a cup in his outstretched hand, a placard hanging from his neck with the words, "I am blind and my dog is dead," the dog lying beside him, all four paws pointed at the sky.

For me, there has been nothing harder to bear than the deaths of my guide dogs, innocent creatures who serve and love. Topper had an inoperable sublingual tumor that caused him great pain. The morning of his last day, Topper and I played in my back yard. He ran as effortlessly as always, fetched the stick and brought it back, dropped it at my feet and stared at it like he did when he was a puppy, but now each time he dropped it, zeal in his eyes, tail wagging, I wished I could die in his place. At the vet's, my arms were around him when his body let go, dropped like a stone, stopped living. His ashes are under a blooming apple tree in our back yard. Tobias, my next dog partner, now lies under a flowering crabapple next to Topper's. The indescribable pain I experienced at each of their deaths strongly suggests that I should seek the alternative, using a white cane instead.

Even though my choices regarding dog guides will never stop the horror of the shortness of canine lives—not until my demise precedes one of theirs—I have wondered about the morality of training dogs to serve humans. Serious dog trainers consider that the rigorous training of the Seeing Eye dog privileges the dog by stretching his capabilities. My gut agrees with this, but my reservation is not the foolish argument hinting at dog enslavement, but my fear that imposing human will upon a dog is based on the biblical, fundamentalist idiocy that preaches man's dominance over all of nature. Once, in New York, I was followed and then chased by a woman yelling, "Free that dog. He is a prisoner, a slave." My belly told me to confront that lunatic, grab her by the throat, but it occurred to me that she might be wielding a knife, not to slit throats but to cut Tobias's harness. The smarter option was to dodge heavy traffic as we flew across Fifty-Seventh Street and ran into the park, the insane lady on our heels.

Separating treacly sentimentality from honoring all life has been a gripping issue. My first wife, Joan, and I followed the bullfights all over Spain. My first time at a village bullring, I threw up. My stomach settled after a few corridas, and eventually my "oles" joined the chorus of thousands. Hemingway's *Death in the Afternoon* guided our bullfight enthusiasms. The medieval pageantry took precedence over my disgust and skepticism about the theatrical metaphors of human domination, allowing me to stomach the maiming and killing of horses and bulls.

In *Adam's Task* and *Animal Happiness*, the trainer, poet, and philosopher Vicki Hearne writes that animals should not be defined by behaviorists' dictates, that in their individuality dogs and horses have the capacity to be in reciprocal relationships with humans both emotionally and morally. To get a better grip on this sacred man-dog relationship, and to be a good partner to a working dog, Hearne insists on the strictest discipline. There are times when I lack the spirit or will to assume the dominance necessary to do my job properly, but if I fail to correct Gabriel properly for a distraction, perhaps a sniff of a dropped crust of pizza or a passing dog's butt, he is smart enough to know that he can get away with it next time, which might be in the middle of a street crossing where it could be a matter of life and death. Stupid, sentimental anthropomorphisms stand between my mawkish tendencies and my obvious needs as a blind man.

The argument favoring the cane over a dog is reasonable. "A cane you can lean against the wall," one of my blind friends told me. "It stays where you put it, no feeding, no fleas, no playtime, no worries."

Rare but terrible things can happen with either cane or dog. A man was walking merrily along a sidewalk with his cane, which did not detect a trailer truck parked across the sidewalk, the steel monster five feet above the street just at the level of his face, which was crushed. Inside the Thirty-Fourth Street subway platform, a woman's dog was suddenly freaked by a noise and jumped up, plunging them both to the tracks. But you don't need to be blind to face the unexpected or to make disastrous mistakes. Nevertheless, how can anyone claim that blindness is a gift, allowing you to experience life in a more profound way? Give me a break. Even worse, my karma-bound friends think that blindness is a payment for past life infringements and an opportunity to look deeper, to think better, to mend one's evil ways. Oy.

3.

A few weeks later, Artur Bobrowski, now our Polish lawyer, flies to New York, rents a car, and drives the four or five hours it takes to get to my house in Vermont. We sit across from each other in the living room, where Gabriel greets our visitor with serious licking. Artur giggles in discomfort and embarrassment, then reaches into his briefcase, finds the proper sheaf of papers, and reads from his printed genealogy, beginning with Joachim David Potok who, born in 1830, married the first of his three wives, with whom he sired eight children; he sired eight more with the second wife, and no one seems to know how many with the third. My line of descent and that of the few surviving Potoks in Australia and England stem from Joachim's first wife, while a distant cousin Anna, who lives in Sweden, is descended from the second.

None of my surviving family talked about the past. I remember my grandmother and my grandfather, my father's parents, but I don't remember most of the many aunts and uncles and cousins. My heart beats faster as Artur, stuttering, reads me name after unknown, unfamiliar name. "B-b-before the war, the property was owned by two brothers, Szewah and Abbe, the last one your great-grandfather," he says. "Szewah's daughter, Rosa Saphier, sold half of the property after the war to a Polish family." I know what he means: Polish as opposed to Jewish, an unbridgeable abyss between the two. "After your great-grandfather's death, still before the war, the other half went to your great-grandmother Sina Prokocimer, born Potok. She died in 1940 in Krakow and her estate was inherited by her children, among them your grandmother Paulina and her brother Wolf." It is almost as if I am listening to a recitation of English kings. Szewa? Abbe? Sina? Wolf? My family? I had never heard names like these before.

I hear Loie turning into our driveway, the car radio blaring. The car door slams, the dog's tail wags, and in she comes. "I will make tea," she says and skips into the kitchen.

"Krakow is a beautiful city," Artur tells Loie as she lays out oatmeal cookies and a pot of Earl Grey with bergamot.

"My father came from Czestochowa," she tells him.

"Yes? Not too far from Krakow. I can arrange a car to take you."

"He came to America in 1920 when he was a little boy, the family driven out by pogrom after pogrom."

"Krakow is on the river Wisla, Vistula to you," Artur says, "a very beautiful river."

"And Andy's family's property?" Loie asks.

"It is not grand," he says, "but well located. We recover it and sell it."

When Artur leaves, we go out hand in hand to the garden Loie has planted in the back of our house. She weeds around the peonies. I stretch out in the hammock, surrounded by the most aromatic flowers—heliotrope, honeysuckle, jasmine—planted here for my benefit. She comes over and describes Artur to me. "He's rather nice looking," she says, "but young, very young."

"This is not a good sign. I would have preferred someone who was old enough to remember the war." I turn to one side to face her. "Also, I hope he's Jewish."

"He could be," Loie says. "But why does that matter?"

"Don't you think that a Jew would really want to stick it to the Poles?"

"Andy," she says, "didn't you listen to the man? You're not going after Poles. Not Poles, not Germans. It's someone in your own family."

2

THE FREDERIC CHOPIN AIRPORT

1.

Mid-March, Loie and I fly to Poland, my third visit since the war, this time not to stimulate memories but to recover property. What does a lefty like me know about property? Once I even believed that property was theft. Still not too sure about that, I'm on my way to claim an apartment house in the name of democracy or justic.

The first and only time I experienced the joy of owning property, it was in the middle of a hundred acres of land, American land, and the house a decrepit Vermont farmhouse, which I enriched over many years with repairs and gifts. Knowing about Jewish property in Poland reverting to Polish Catholics, its "rightful owners," in my gut I suspected that this pristine American hundred acres was only temporarily mine and would find its way back to the pilgrim Christian farmers to whom it truly belonged. In fact, after thirty years of ownership, my house, fields, and forests were lost in divorce, then sold to strangers. My trees, fences, barns, and soil, my American soil, I replaced nearly twenty years ago with the turn-of-the-last-century Dutch Colonial house that Loie and I live in on Richardson Street in Montpelier, with its old dark paneling, its carpeted staircase, the landing with the bay windows, even the sunlight I no longer see, which floods the rooms facing south.

This return to Poland is my first with not a shred of eyesight. When I was there in the late 1980s, the Warsaw airport looked like a converted cow barn, filthy and smelly. The immigration processing had been as dependent on the mood of the little functionaries whose power was exercised by their willingness to use that life-or-death rubber stamp, probably the same one they used at the Lithuanian border in 1939. A new airport, named after Frederic Chopin, has been built since my last visit, just before the end of the Communist occupation. Loie describes it as a run-of-the-mill modern building, a grade or two above the Stalinist architecture I had described to her before our arrival. Inside Frederic Chopin, we stand with hundreds of others in a long line, awaiting the stamping of our passports. Our flight to Krakow is scheduled to take off in an hour.

"They slammed the door shut up ahead and our line is not moving at all," Loie says and pulls me into another line. But we're in jolly Poland where apparatchiks have been empowered by generations of ineptitude and the freedom to call untimely coffee breaks. Behind us, nervous mumbles begin. Inching forward minute by painful minute, we are herded toward security. It is now fifteen minutes until our Krakow connection. We don't have the cell phone number of Artur's representative, Basia, who awaits us at Pope John Paul II, Krakow's main airport. "The next plane after ours," Loie reads from the flight directory on a wall, "is in five hours," making me sweat and breathe faster. I want to push my way to the front of the line to yell at the security guy.

"If I could see I'd kill the son of a bitch," I spit out from my clenched teeth.

"No you wouldn't," she says.

"Find him for me." She says nothing. I think: "Fuck, fuck, fuck." I turn back toward the people behind us, colleagues in oppression. If I were an orchestra conductor—a career I once considered—I would bring them to a crashing crescendo, a nightmarish roar. The mumbling rises in pitch. I begin to shake. "Krakow, Krakow," I yell, pronouncing it in English, then Polish. My body is out of control. I'm an eight-year-old again, about to cross a different border, this time coming into Poland instead of racing to get out. I'm in full panic attack mode. The beating of my heart shakes my chest, numbs my hands.

"Stop it, Andy," Loie warns. "You're going to have a heart attack."

Suddenly someone yanks my white cane from my hands. What comes out of my mouth is dog-like, a growl. "That's my leather coat," I yell, "My backpack." Someone—the security asshole or Loie—grabs them from me and the people in line behind us are silenced.

Loie pulls me toward her. "They are not thrilled with your drama," she whispers. "If you don't stop, they're going to put you away."

"It's the same fucking Poles," I growl into her ear.

"No, it's not," Loie says quietly. "Different Poles. Very different." She puts an arm around me.

"These fuckers control my life." I open my mouth to scream but I can't. I hate myself for not screaming. I hate myself for wanting to scream. Memories and messages abound in my sub-cortical, subliminal mind, some from my mother's world of propriety and clean underpants, some from a more heroic time in my life, from a large canvas of reds and blacks and yellows, some from the huge sculptures in a green summer meadow. Loie helps me on with my coat, and the apparatchik fuckhead shoves my cane back into my hands. Loie and I run for the Krakow connection.

2.

Of the 732 Jewish boys approximately my age whom Holocaust historian Martin Gilbert interviewed for his book *The Boys*, none came from a background like mine: privileged, urban, cosmopolitan, free of religion. Amazingly, they all survived the abuse of the Poles and the German death camps and were able to recall their unspeakable experiences with composure and intelligence. Their pre-war existence, whether rural or urban, took place among other Jewish children, all of them subjected to strict religious studies. Christian boys beat on them every chance they had. "Soon after the capitulation of Warsaw," one man wrote from England fifty years later, "the Germans set up field kitchens to serve the population, who were starved as a result of the siege which had lasted a few weeks. As the queue formed for the soup, the soldiers started shouting 'Juden raus.' But often, they could not tell who was Jewish and found help from the Polish youngsters who went round pointing out the Jews." Would anyone have pointed me out? I didn't even know I was Jewish. Did everyone else know? "What hurt most," the man continued, "was the fact that the boy who pointed at me was the same boy with whom I had worked a few weeks ago building barricades at the top of our street. And my father and uncle were still in the Polish army."

Compared with The Boys, my scars of war are minor, though they didn't seem minor at the time. In July of 1939, I spent my eighth birthday walking in a beautiful field of wild flowers with my grandmother Paulina. Late in the afternoon, the sky turned crimson and my grandmother squeezed my hand and whispered that this was a sign that war was coming.

A month later, the German foreign minister, Ribbentrop, and the Soviet foreign minister, Molotov, signed a non-aggression pact. A week after that, a little before dawn of September 1, I was racing, flying, on the new English bicycle, black and sleek, that my Uncle Max had brought from London. I was laughing like a crazy boy. The speed was exhilarating, the air rushing through my hair, through my whole body. I yelped and threw my head back as I floated over the bumps and stones on the field across from Max's newly built summerhouse, some sixteen kilometers north of Warsaw. I removed my hands from the handlebars and laughed, screaming with joy, as loud as I could, then closed my eyes for moments at a time. I flew in the sky like a bird. My whole body trembled with joy, a whooping, crazy, total joy. And then, three airplanes appeared just over the treetops, the red and white checkerboard Polish insignia painted on their wings, so low that I could see the pilots' faces in their hoods and masks. I knew that they were flying to bomb Hitler. So much happiness. My heart beat faster. Their wings shone silver as the sun began to lighten the dark sky. What a morning it was. I dropped the bicycle at my feet, puffed out my chest, and saluted. But the Polish insignia was a lie, and the German Junker planes began to dive, their Jericho trumpets screaming, a horrible howling sound, and bombs slipped out from each of them, exploding all over the field. The stones and clods of earth and fire that hit me on my chest and back and legs abolished one world, my childhood, and introduced me to the rest of my life. Trees exploded and the field I knew so well was sucked dry of air. The planes droned on as if nothing had happened, but I couldn't stop screaming. The me of eight years of life was blown out of existence.

Probably no more than a few weeks later, W. H. Auden wrote a poem he called "September 1, 1939":

> I sit in one of the dives
> On Fifty-second Street
> Uncertain and afraid

As the clever hopes expire
Of a low dishonest decade:
Waves of anger and fear
Circulate over the bright
And darkened lands of the earth,
Obsessing our private lives;
The unmentionable odour of death
Offends the September night.

Accurate scholarship can
Unearth the whole offence
From Luther until now
That has driven a culture mad,
Find what occurred at Linz,
What huge imago made
A psychopathic god:
I and the public know
What all schoolchildren learn,
Those to whom evil is done
Do evil in return. . . .

Later that day, Max drove us back to Warsaw, soon to be leveled by bombs. Much of my family gathered in my parents' apartment to decide on their next move. I was allowed to stay up while they talked late into the night. Under the dining room table playing with my toy soldiers, I listened to the outbursts, the tears, the scraping of the chairs, and the shuffling of feet. My mother said quietly, "Men and children go. I stay."

"I won't go without you," I cried from under the table, speaking up for the first and only time. The radio played the Polish national anthem. I could not stand up as I always did when the chorus sang. "The British and French will come to our defense if the Germans attack," the radio announcer said and I moved a column of my soldiers to a border of the Persian rug.

"Yes, yes, they will come," my father said, and my uncle Max yelled at him, calling him an idiot. My uncle Stash then yelled at Max, using a word that made me blush.

"How long can it take before the monster is crushed?" my grandfather Solomon asked. "The French army is the strongest in Europe, and Britain rules the seas," my mother's sister Eva said.

The French offer was not a bluff. They did declare war on Germany but they were in no position to provide serious help. Poland itself had a million-man army and another million in the reserves, not nearly enough.

What went through my family's minds? Did they know the true risks? Having been alive during the previous war, could they envisage what was about to happen? They must have assured one another that a slaughter like that could never happen again. On the other hand, they might have been sensitive to the human capacity for folly and evil. Our apartment was safe, full of lovely furniture, damask draperies, a baby grand piano, an old grandfather clock. But they read the newspapers. Surely they knew that next door in Germany, as early as 1933, anti-Semitism was beginning to be enforced by law? What about in 1935 when the Nuremberg laws prohibited German citizenship for Jews? As I played in the Warsaw parks, did they not hear the glass crashing on Kristallnacht? Why did they wait so long? Even in Germany, by the start of the war, around 250,000 of 437,000 German Jews had emigrated to the United States and Palestine. Many of my family's friends in Poland emigrated during the 1930s. How unwelcome did my mother and uncle feel as they continued to design and sell fur coats? Polish policy, well known to all, was not to kill Jews but to get them off Polish soil to Palestine. The German plan was to starve all the Slavs as well as the Jews, the former because Slavs were racially inferior, sub-human; the latter a step worse than sub-human. Jews did not even make the grade. They were non-human.

My family must have heard of the Germans screaming about *lebensraum*, proclaiming that, as the Aryan master race, they were forced, no, entitled to expand eastward where the inferior races lived. Didn't my family realize that they were members of the most hated of the inferior races? They lived just one country east of Germany.

As I was growing up, did my parents worry about their happy little Jewish son playing in the Warsaw parks, supervised by his Catholic governesses? While I gamboled through my peaceful childhood, didn't the fear of Jew hatred cloud their assimilated existence? Did they consider leaving the country or did they simply put it off until airplanes above us made German intentions clear?

As I try to comprehend what makes some people leave everything behind, and when it becomes clear that the moment to flee is now, I'm awed by my family's decision to leave, even late, and to accomplish the leaving as successfully as they did in spite of all the odds against them. How wrenchingly, impossibly hard it must have been to let go of their beautiful apartments, factories, and houses in Bedzin, a thriving business in Warsaw, the new suits bought on Savile Row in London, the dresses from the House of Worth, the Empire furniture, all those precious fur coats. Saying good-bye to home, comfort, daily life, and language requires the acceptance of unheard-of risk, a huge jump into the unknown.

Is it only the rich who had such choices? It is unlikely that poor people without connections could have done it, especially as late as a week into September of 1939. One would have needed cars, money for bribes, contacts in other countries, some knowledge about the world. And then, rich or poor, who can ever be sure if a present danger will or will not blow over and life will or will not resume as before? Now, eighty years later, there may be people in America who don't want to live inside the belly of this beast, with its ultranationalism, right-wing populism, the fervor of ignorant fundamentalism, the glaring inequality, and a policy of endless war. A rich person can buy a condo in Canada; the rest can only hope for change, a return to democracy.

One day in the 1920s when the writer Stefan Zweig was traveling in Germany with a friend, the two men visited an exhibition of antique furniture at a museum in Munich. Zweig stopped in front of a display of enormous medieval wooden chests. "Can you tell me," he asked, "which of these chests belonged to Jews?" To his friend, they all looked to be of equally high quality, with no apparent marks of identification. Zweig smiled. "Do you see these two here? They are mounted on wheels. They belonged to Jews." He went on to explain: "In those days, as indeed always! the Jewish people were never sure when the whistle would blow, when the rattles of pogrom would creak. They had to be ready to flee at a moment's notice."

I have no idea if my family thought of themselves as Jews who had long been targeted by Germany for destruction, or as Poles whose country was being bombed. In school we made paper gas masks, a crafts project, and a few days before Germans crossed the border into Poland, I jumped with glee on my bed as the radio played a song, "May Cholera Take Hitler," and sprained my ankle. Except for a child's mindless patriotism, I was clueless. But did they suspect that a German invasion meant not only the conquest of their country, but also the annihilation of the Jews? That should not have been merely a suspicion. They were educated. Even if the Polish newspapers did not tell the entire truth of events in Germany and Austria and Czechoslovakia, they must have heard of the Anschluss in Austria

25

or the destruction of Jewish lives and property during Kristallnacht in 1938. As we raced for the border, did they think of themselves only as Poles, as Polish Jews, or just as Jews? I was unaware of Jewishness as a concept or identification, and I wonder if they realized what their fate would have been as Jews had they failed.

3.

In 1979 I traveled from Paris to Poland, my first time back since the war. Though I had studied and worked in Paris for several years, boarding a train bound for Warsaw had never occurred to me before. Best to leave it alone, I'd thought, best not to tempt the night terrors. But 1979 was the fortieth anniversary of the beginning of my war and the end of my charmed childhood. I boarded a train from the Gare du Nord. Uncle Max's daughter, my cousin Anita, so close to me that we consider each other brother and sister, was going to meet me in Warsaw a couple of days after my arrival. She was six and I was eight when we got out of Poland in 1939, and our memories of the war sometimes differed. Her interest, like mine, is to piece it together as best we can, though we both acknowledge the unreliability of memory and try to honor each other's version.

Until the train crossed into Germany, I was happy to flex my French language muscles in conversation with a middle-aged Parisian couple. In the morning, the train stopped on the outskirts of Berlin. Our car was shunted to a sidetrack, awaiting, I supposed, a new locomotive. I thought about my mother, who two months before the war began had traveled to Paris for the fall collections. Coco Chanel urged her to return to Poland earlier than she had planned. "Madame Coco told me," my mother said, "that I must rescue my son when the war begins." She had to be urged?

And by a virulent anti-Semite like the famous Coco? It doesn't seem possible that during the summer of 1939 my mother felt secure enough to make a business trip through Germany, but she did manage to get on the train back to Warsaw, the same Paris-Warsaw train I was on and, just like mine, her train stopped in Berlin. "I try to be invisible," she told me. "I was so afraid that Germans take me off the train and look in my passport which says I am Jewish." But not only did my mother go to Paris in 1939, but Uncle Max had flown to New York earlier that year to exhibit Apfelbaum's furs in the Polish Pavilion of the World's Fair.

A fellow passenger on my Warsaw-bound train informed me that we were in a Berlin suburb called Wannsee. Oh my God, not Wannsee! I stood up and shivered. This is where, in 1942, at the so-called Wannsee Conference, Reinhard Heydrich, the SS-Obergruppenfuhrer whom Hitler called "the man with the iron heart," together with the elite German High Command, first proclaimed "the Final Solution," the destruction of European Jews. My stomach began to hurt. Forty years after the Wannsee Conference, in Christian Democratic Germany, I feared for my life, Germany being Germany. Our railway car stood quietly for hours. Like my mother, I dared not look out the window, dared not move. I awoke as we sped toward the Polish border, rumbling from the frying pan into the fire.

The Warsaw Central Station felt familiar, not that I remembered its dungeon-like echoes, but surely my governess and I stood on this platform, then boarded trains to the mountains or the seashore. My mother must have walked this platform; my father may have come to meet her; my grandparents must have walked where I now walked, their shoes squeaking as they boarded their train back to Bedzin.

During my first eight years, 375,000 Jews lived here in Warsaw, one-third of the total population. Now a few thousand remained. In the street outside the station, once alive with horse-drawn buggies, there were no *doroczkas*, no comforting smell of horse manure. A taxi drove me to the Hotel Europejski where my uncle Stash used to take me some Sundays for cocoa and cakes. Once elegant, the lobby was squalid now, smelling of cabbage and mold.

A day later, Anita arrived. We roamed the city partially rebuilt from the rubble of the 1939 German bombings (the devastation equal to that of Dresden, fire bombed by Allied planes during the war) and from the total house by house German destruction during the ill-fated Warsaw Uprising of 1944 as the Soviet Army waited patiently across the Vistula for the job to be done. Since then, parts of the city were reconstructed according to old plans and paintings, and much of the rest rebuilt in the cheap ugly Soviet style architecture. Not only did the city seem depleted of energy, but the people wandering in the streets looked gray and lifeless. Anita and I walked into the Saski Gardens, where the sensuality that accompanied me for the rest of my life was born. I remembered the ladies sitting on park benches, their hands inside fur muffs, watching as I scoured the ground for the spiky green meaty shell that contained the treasure, the slippery glossy horse chestnut. Now the gardens looked desolate and barren. A path led past the Tomb of the Unknown Soldier with its little eternal flame, and I spat, hating all allusions to heroes, patriots, warriors.

Number Four Moniuszki, where I was born and lived until the beginning of the war, was still standing, though pockmarked with bullet holes and listing to one side. "Let's go in," Anita said, but when we pushed and tugged at the large wooden front door, it did not budge. No one went in or out. I tried to imagine myself wheeled by governesses in my baby carriage until I could walk and pump the pedals of my tricycle, the boy who jumped and skipped and ran, yelped, hummed, and jabbered. But nothing here stimulated my memory. Nothing looked the way it had. In front of an adjoining building, in worse shape than Number Four, a wreath of flowers had been left, "in honor of some fucking apparatchik," a friend later told us. We took a short walk to one end of Moniuszki, which opens into the once-splendid boulevard, Marszalkowska. Flattened by the Germans, it was now in the shadow of the hideous Palace of Culture, Stalin's gift to the Warsaw he helped destroy, the gift as welcome as a hemorrhoid. A short distance from this monstrosity, Apfelbaum's, the family business, once stood proudly among other smart, elegant shops, the crown jewel of European fur salons, beautifully appointed with Persian carpets and satin couches, the walls hung with silver sconces, a gorgeous ironwork French elevator transporting royalty to the showrooms above. Marszalkowska was a haven, and their salon a place of sumptuous, luxurious objects I loved to touch. There at Apfelbaum's, I was shown off, patted and praised by workers in the factory, and salesmen and models in the showrooms. Right from the beginning, I was eager for adulation, always prepared to smile, though the charm that served me badly most of my life has now been supplanted by anger and revenge fantasies.

Anita and I hired a taxi to take us to Wieliszew, about sixteen kilometers north of Warsaw where, forty years earlier, on the first day of the war, three German planes had dropped their bombs all around me. Once in the village, we didn't know how to direct our driver to the site; we knew only that the house stood alone, surrounded by fields and forests. The taxi stopped arbitrarily, trees to one side, a plowed field on the other. Somewhere near us was the spot where I once stood, my bicycle at my feet, and saluted three Junker dive bombers, or whatever they were. Anita and I were desperate for a marker, the remains of a structure, a foundation, a garden gate, but there was nothing, no sense of home, not here, not in Warsaw, no hint of a visual memory.

A stooped old woman appeared at one end of the mown field and walked toward us, dragging a scythe behind her. When she stepped onto the road, I asked in my nearly forgotten Polish if she remembered where a summerhouse or two had been before the war. She looked us up and down. "The Jews." She showed her teeth and spat. "That's where the Jews lived," she barked and went on her way, transforming my melancholy to fury. I had wanted a few bricks, a corner of a roof, broken cement, and I got a shot of virulent Jew hatred as never before in my adult life. Searching for life-changing mementos seemed to be a dead end.

How immensely different were the stories of the few surviving members of my family. One of my cousins, another Anita, this one living in London, five years younger than I, was taken with her parents to a camp in the Soviet Union at the beginning of the war. Her diplomat father was treated more kindly than most of the Polish Jews incarcerated in dread Russia. Sick from malnutrition, she spent months in the camp hospital. After four and a half years in the Soviet camp, they were allowed to go back to their residence in Sosnowiec, an industrial city not far from Bedzin, where they stayed for the next four years. In Sosnowiec, where all the Jews had been herded into a ghetto and subsequently sent to Auschwitz, eleven-year-old Anita witnessed a large crowd of Poles shouting and throwing stones at the few returning Jews, the terrifying scene becoming an old-fashioned pogrom, the kind that had plagued Jews in this part of the world for generations, not only in Poland but in all the countries of Central and Eastern Europe. Very frightened, Anita ran home and, a short time later, her father, on an economic mission in London, applied and was granted political asylum. She was fourteen and a half when she began her new life in England.

4.

In 1988, the year before Solidarity took over from the apparatchiks, with the city still glum, joyless, and gray, my ex-wife Charlotte, my first Seeing Eye dog Dash, my son Mark and I went to Warsaw, my last time until now. The police goons were still cracking skulls, the intelligentsia just coming out of prison or hiding. We met many smart and politically engaged people. One of them, a prominent activist in the Solidarity movement, explained Polish collaboration in the destruction of Polish Jews by saying, "People do crazy things during Holocausts." I couldn't believe what I had just heard and didn't know what to say. After an uncomfortable pause, I asked if she was Jewish. "Yes," she said, "but you must understand that really I am Polish." I understood well because my super-assimilated parents considered themselves Poles and believed in the Polish values of gallantry, honor, and patriotism, and looked down on shtetl Jews as dirty country people who didn't speak Polish but rather that ugly language called Yiddish and lived in the stupidity of pre-industrial rituals and laws.

But "crazy during Holocausts?" It didn't compute. "Crazy is a disgusting modifier of people who lived through the Holocaust," my son said as we walked back to our rented apartment.

Next on the list of interesting people recommended by a writer friend who was fascinated by Polish history was a non-Jewish, Polish woman who, by reputation, was not an anti-Semite. "You see," she said as we drank tea in her crowded little apartment, "in our Polish house, we were

Jews and Poles living together. When the Germans came, we Poles helped our kind first. It's only natural."

"I see. It was ours and yours. So after you helped yours, you tried to help ours? How did you do that?"

"You'd be surprised how many of us helped the Jews," she said and offered us slices of a cake she baked for the occasion. I wanted to say that I was surprised how many did not, but said nothing. "What would you do," she rightfully asked, "if you faced certain death if even suspected of helping a Jew?"

The moral rectitude of risking one's life by helping another is unquestionable, a reason to believe in the possibility of true heroism. I wonder what I would have done in their place. I wish I could be sure of my answer. At this point in my life, I think I could act heroically. But what if I were young, even in middle age? In the lists of the righteous at Yad Vashem, Poland, with more than six thousand righteous, has the largest number among all nations. The number who helped send Jews to the death camps is not available, nor is the number of bystanders who did not care one way or the other.

Another day, we sat in the comfortable library of one of the important political dissenters, one of the few who returned to his Jewish roots. A yarmulke on his head, he told us that Polish anti-Semitism was no worse than French Jew hatred or anyone else's, "but in Poland," he said, "it is not disreputable. It is taken for granted."

"You make it sound almost civilized," I told him.

"I am in a bus, the yarmulke on my head, and I hear a group of young people discuss what this is on top of my head. One of them explains and then they stare at me as if I were a Zulu. Of course, they have heard of Jews from their parents but they've never seen one," he told us, "and that is why I stay in Poland."

A few moments of silence followed. I looked down at my hands and tried to understand the courage, compassion, and patience it must have taken to decide to live his life this way. "The anti-Semitism doesn't bother you?" I finally asked.

"I can't say that I like it," he said.

"I've hardly ever experienced anti-Semitism in America. I don't know why I feel that it's in the air here in Poland."

He seemed surprised, and I thought that perhaps I was just another paranoid Jew, ready to explode at the merest suggestion that someone does not like me. "Just because someone says he does not like Jews or a particular Jew," he said, "it does not mean that he's an anti-Semite." We shuffled in our chairs. "Absolutely not," he said. "I don't like most Germans but that does not mean that I'm anti-German."

I didn't get it then and I still don't. How many Germans does one have to hate to be an anti-German? Still, I'm not at all sure why I have become such a defender of the Jews, why I am so sensitive to every slight, every rumor, hint, or possibility of a slight. I didn't learn it at home. Nothing Jewish was admitted to Moniuszki Four, not the cooking, not the cooks, not the unassimilated. In their fancy fur salon, strangely left with its unabashedly Jewish name, Apfelbaum's, the showroom staff, the dapper salesmen, sleek models with little breasts and noses, were anything but Jewish. The Warsaw gentry would not have tolerated big noses or tits.

Toward the end of my last visit twenty-five years ago, I asked our taxi driver to take us to a school for small blind children. He could not believe what he heard. "Blind children, Mr. Andrew? You want to visit blind children?" When he parked on the edge of a lovely woods called Laski, he again told us that it was beyond his understanding that anyone would want to witness something as depressing as blind children. He turned the radio on to American country music and reached for his newspaper. "You must come back quickly," he said.

Inside the simple building, we were met by one of the nuns who ran the place. When she opened the door to the large playroom, we were treated with happy squeals. Dozens of little kids were playing with large balls, blocks, and metal slides, and their laughter drowned the sad mood of everything else in Poland. Then one of the nuns gathered the kids to explain what my guide dog does. "This is Dash," she said. "He helps Mr. Andrew walk in the streets." In my very bad Polish, I tried to tell them that I hoped they would one day have a dog to help them too. The nun said something after I finished, undoubtedly translating my words into an acceptable Polish. All the children made an oooh sound that could only mean "how wondrous the world."

"Do not be afraid of the dog," the nun said, "and those who want to pet Dash, make a line starting right here behind Jacek." One by one, they stroked my dog carefully, very carefully. These storybook nuns and children gave us the sweetest moment of our entire stay in Poland.

That was in 1988. No such luck this time.

3

HOTEL HELENA RUBINSTEIN

1.

"So," Loie says now as we settle into the Hotel Rubinstein in the old Jewish section of Krakow, "are you surprised you had a panic attack at the airport?"

"Embarrassed, the stereotypical ugly American."

"PTSD," says my psychologist wife. "It's all that old stuff coming back." She hangs up our coats in the closet. "Plus blindness," she adds.

"Picture this," I say. "Disembodied voices come at me as in a nightmare."

"It's the cognitive brain—your reason—which turns off and all you have left is the very old feeling," Loie says.

Maybe so, I am thinking, but there's also this: the once defenseless child as bombs fell around him is now the man who cannot defend himself because he cannot see. Not seeing, a thick, soundless blanket of fear sometimes hovers about me, a dark cloud, a tremor in the ground. But here, there's not only that, but also the vulnerability and fear of a Jew returning to Poland. "I never feel as Jewish as here," I tell Loie.

"I know," she says. "It drove my father and his parents

out of here when he was a little boy." She sits down to rest. "But the only anti-Semitism I ever felt in my life was growing up in Westchester County, both in school and from the parents of school friends."

Before Loie, I thought PTSD was just a trendy Vermont badge of honor, trauma perhaps being one in a list of things awaiting serenity prayers. Everyone was recovering from some damn thing or another. Not me. I was in charge of me, no dipshit recovery needed here; but now post-traumatic stress disorder is supposed to be taking its place as one of the central themes of my life. Surely a tirade of emotion might support a diagnostic rationale, but the moment of such anger, such a desire for revenge, does not always hearken back to childhood pain. The fear of a group's hatred of one's kind is surely reason enough for rage, which is certainly more fitting than forgiveness.

At first it was called shell shock, the explanations supposed at the time to be certain and complete by almost everyone, including the headmasters of boarding schools I was sent to, where I often awoke screaming in terror. We arrived in New York in February 1940, and it must have been later in that month, or March at the latest, when someone—who knows who?—drove me across the East River to an Ethical Culture School in Brooklyn. With no English language, bombs still bursting in my head, I was alone in what must have seemed like Alaska—though I had never heard of Alaska. With a group of other boys, I was put out onto a freezing porch where, like brave warriors, we were to spend the night. The sheets were starched and icy, the door into the house closed. I must have fallen asleep and awoke screaming, the first of my black black nightmares. An ink black sky, a thick, dense blackness, closed in on me like an iron vise. Nothing could stop it. It was the end. It was massive, inexorable, an implosion of the universe. I screamed and screamed. My eyes opened and I didn't know where I was. A woman was talking to me in a language I barely recognized while the other boys peeked out from under their bed covers. With my few words of English, I wanted them to see the airplanes that bombed me. Every one of them strained to listen. I didn't know if they understood as I somehow came up with a story in Polish mixed with sound effects and theatrical gestures about a brother who tucked a hand grenade into his belly and threw himself under a German tank. My hunger for sympathy must have been voracious, and I have no idea where the brother story came from. Eventually, everything settled on the freezing porch and, happily, I did not sleep another night in Brooklyn.

How could I not love the next place they sent me to, the Hudson School, a mansion and a few other buildings in a wooded part of New Rochelle, not far from the city. I greeted the sight of the big old houses and lawns with relief, sensing the possibility of belonging. Here, finally, was safety and solace, a place for me to discover the growing American in me, away from my distraught family, also struggling for a foothold in New York.

Not long after stepping into New York from the Bergensfjord and Ellis Island, I numbed out not only the sounds of bombs and bullets—all the terrors that soon found a home in my nightmares—but also the hugs and laughter of my family, of Solomon and Paulina, my long-dead grandparents. In all the schools I was sent to in America, I was the only one who didn't have grandparents.

Even the American war became my war. Guadalcanal, not Auschwitz, not Treblinka, not Majdanek. While my war destroyed my family and home, I sat at the dining table of my little boarding school in New Rochelle, eating sweet sections of canned pineapple, listening to the swing and sway of Sammy Kaye.

At that wonderful little school, nurtured by its teachers and accepted by schoolmates, I sculpted a clay panther and glazed it black. Everyone told me that it was a marvel. Where did this panther come from? Mimicry of the world of objects and words? My body craved the language and the art. Nothing was more central to my existence.

My concentration focused on becoming American, taking charge, cutting the language bonds that tied me to my father and mother who, in their forties, were slow to learn English and spoke with heavy accents. I wonder now if my swallowing the English language whole in one great gulp was as much an act of defiance as one of self-preservation and a desperate rage for a new identity. Apparently, until the age of twelve, a child's brain is wired to receive such enormous gifts as language. Suddenly, my hard Polish Rs were replaced by back-of-the-throat vowel-like American Rs, and my parents laughed when my Polish began to be compromised by softer Ls.

Even though my first eight years were happy ones, I have only one childhood memory of my mother. She had walked home from Apfelbaum's in the middle of one day and stood with my governess in the hallway, awaiting my bowel movement as I sat in the small WC, straining to produce. When I emerged triumphant, she was there in her cold mink coat, fresh from the Warsaw winter. I must have, at one time or another, been in her arms, fed by her, maybe even taken into her bed and hugged, but I don't remember any such occasion.

I didn't realize how abnormal the lack of body contact between mother and son was until, at the age of ten or so, at the Hudson School, a boy named Stevie who lived in Massachusetts invited me to his home for a weekend. His father picked us up and we drove through unknown landscapes and arrived in a driveway with green grass on either side. A woman, his mother, ran out to greet us. She wrapped her arms around us both, startling me. Inside the house, all the lamps were on, making everything yellow and orange.

My shoes sank into carpets so thick that it felt like walking on pillows. Stevie's mama touched us, hugged us, and sang songs, I think in Italian. That night I woke up screaming as the universe, which took up the whole sky, descended on me, its enormous steel vise about to crush me, crush the whole collapsing world. I screamed and screamed, then felt the softness of a woman's body: Stevie's mama held me in her arms, rocking me and singing softly. I was enveloped by her warm, soft breasts, alive again and sleepy. Though I never saw Stevie or his family again, I will never forget that weekend, always yearning to re-create the loveliness of soft large women and breasts.

This was a very different warmth than the kind offered by my mother. Still, my mother and my uncle Max were the power in the family. They made things happen, while my father stewed and moaned, crying out for the help he never got, except, perhaps, during those weeks in Poland and America that he spent at various sanatoriums, places that furnished rest from contempt, the freedom to smile. I gravitated to the power, joining his oppressors not from cruelty, but self-preservation. Who knows the pain my mother suffered because of her husband's malice and parsimony? Only in retrospect do I feel pity as well as sympathy, and even admiration for their ability to survive war, displacement, a new life begun in their forties, and, above all, each other.

Even though Uncle Max drove us out of the war to safety, it was my mother, a few inches shorter than five feet tall, who, in her quiet way, took charge when both Max and my father wanted to go back to Warsaw. She drove Max on, cajoling and flattering as she pursed her lips, looking straight ahead, not blinking, immovable. She and her brother rose to the occasion, Max yelling and complaining all the way, she insisting on "only New York."

My mother lived her happiest years after Max then my father, Leon, died—my uncle in 1953, my father in 1966.

More than twenty years of non-interference from their anger and depression allowed her to live quietly, work hard, buy the furniture and paintings she loved and could afford without being yelled at, and give of herself generously and fully, especially to me. She lived until the age of ninety and died free of pain or chronic illness. For no apparent reason, she decided to stay in bed from the time she stopped working in her late eighties. She believed she would join her brother in her version of heaven, which was probably ruled by the Old Testament God but may also have included images she received from a devout Catholic nurse who visited her once every two weeks to administer a vitamin B12 injection and talk to her about Jesus. One such time, I watched as my mother listened with pious intent to yet another Jesus tale, her eyes bright, her mouth open, looking like Bernini's *Ecstasy of Saint Teresa*.

Though she told everyone that she was quite ready to die, she ate a banana a day on her Upper East Side doctor's insistence to ensure her daily intake of potassium. The night she died, more than twenty years after my father, I had flown down from Vermont to visit as I'd been doing every few weeks. Before I left for the evening, I went into her bedroom where she and her housekeeper, Emma, were watching the New York Philharmonic on television. I kissed her cheek and took a cab uptown to a friend's book party. When I came back late in the evening, all was quiet and I went to bed in the guest room. Before dawn, Emma, near hysterics, woke me and led me into my mother's bedroom where she lay on her bed, her hands folded under her breasts, no longer breathing. Soon, the funeral people wheeled a gurney into her bedroom, covered her, and strapped her body to the gurney. I stood and watched. The act of carrying her small sturdy body and laying straps across it was a violation of that small strong woman, an act that made no sense. They then rolled the beloved Madame

Potok into the long hallway on the seventeenth floor, waited for the elevator and, as morning traffic sped up and down Fifty-Seventh Street, transferred my mother's body into the back of their hearse.

Among the people who gathered in her apartment a few days after her death was a long-forgotten first PR lady hired by Maximilian Furs in the 1940s. As if she had never left the scene, she gushed about the arrival in New York of the Potoks and Apfelbaums. "I shall never forget this family," said Rosemary, still the consummate PR liar. She cooed, "Not long after their arrival in New York, Madame and her fabulous brother, Monsieur Michel Maximilian, with their beautiful children next to them, sat like royalty among their fabulous minks, chinchillas, and sables."

"What is that woman talking about?" I asked Anita who stood next to me, her mouth wide open, unbelieving. "We got off the goddam boat and lived in some Upper West Side hovel."

My mother was a saint according to some of her friends and customers, always generous with advice, gifts of flowers, effusive compliments, always ready to take on discomfort in order to ease someone else's burden.

2.

Some evenings in that love fest of a Hudson School, we kids sat on the plush carpet in the living room and our teachers talked to us about the sky, the earth, the birth of cities, often ending with requests for my drawings, which earned the love of the little girls and even teachers. "I'll trade you for a panther," one of my little girlfriends whispered and, though I could not duplicate the ceramic panther, I did draw one and she let me stick my hand inside her shirt. Another little girl invited me to watch her pee for a picture of an apple tree in bloom.

When I told Loie about being coddled, loved, and praised for whatever qualities were discovered in me, and how drawing had come to me in what seemed like a single inhalation, she said, "You sly dog. How old were you anyway?"

"Maybe ten or eleven. But you should have seen the panther."

"I think that getting laid is the reason most artists paint," Loie said.

While I cavorted at the Hudson School, the grownups remade their fur business on Fifty-Seventh Street. After my two years in New Rochelle, my mother was advised by one of her new rich customers to send me to "a serious school." I was shipped off to the Williston Junior School in East Hampton, Massachusetts, where my nightmares reappeared with a vengeance. They were soothed regularly by Mrs. Clare, the headmaster's wife. She sat at the side of my bed and gently laid cool washcloths on my forehead. Some nights that year, I awoke knowing that terror was coming and tried to erase it by walking the halls of the dormitory. But I could not stop it. I saw no airplanes or bombs, but only a black abstraction deleting the universe.

In the middle of that first New England winter, I woke up one night, sat up in bed, and looked out the frosted window into the snow-covered street, lit by a single street lamp. My aloneness was sharply defined by the cold, the snow, the silence, the empty street. The scene outside the window was a reflection of me, a me that didn't belong, not in East Hampton, Massachusetts, not with my parents in New York, not in my blue room on Moniuszki Street, not anywhere. From that night, aloneness and otherness were hardwired in my identity, taking their place among the well-learned social graces. At times loneliness surfaced as comfort, a home of its own, a center around which the panorama of my life unwound.

I lived for more than seventy years relatively numb to the past, but now the past is forcing me to confront it, baiting me with, of all things, real estate.

3.

The Hotel Rubinstein was named for Helena Rubinstein, the twentieth-century cosmetics queen, who grew up in a house in the neighborhood. In post-war Poland, a smart entrepreneur named a hotel after her, understanding that Jewish names and the refurbishing of old synagogues and cemeteries would become rewarding tourist bait. Although all the Jews of Kazimierz were exterminated, Jews remain a valuable financial resource. Remarkably, Helena Rubinstein was the person who, already very rich, bought the first fur coat from my mother's Maximilian Furs in New York and thus helped her launch a successful business.

I find it strange that my mother and uncle's business in Warsaw was named Apfelbaum, their name, but when they opened their salon in New York, they renamed it. A Jewish name in pre-war Warsaw was okay. In supposedly tolerant America, Apfelbaum would never have made it to the top. I guess they wanted to begin fresh. Regarding anti-Semitism, they would take no more chances.

Loie turns to one side in bed and begins to purr softly while I listen for sounds of Poland, a man in the courtyard below speaking Polish, the sound of a car navigating the snowy streets as American country music blares on the car radio. I try to distinguish between seeing a little, as I did on my last visit, to seeing nothing now. Last time, I had to move my head left or right or up in order to avoid the large central blind spot that was spreading over my field of vision. Still, though blurrier, the Saski Gardens and Lazienki Park were pretty much the same as they had been when I was a child. The child's excitement was missing, but a kind of

43

shadowy layout and the architecture of the parks, fleeting and spotty as an after-image, appeared briefly on my retinas. The feeling of no longer belonging has become greater without the momentary distraction of a pretty face or a flower provided by eyesight. Without that, I am left with my frustration, my revenge fantasies, my aversion to those Poles—certainly not all, but many too many—who consider the purity of their Christian nation sullied by the likes of any "other," which includes me and people like me.

"Blindness is as dead as an end can be," I grumble to Loie in the morning.

"Wrong again," she says, just out of the shower. "You've been a great model for others, and that's what keeps it from being a dead end."

"For you, the glass is always half full," I say as we stretch our jet-lagged bones. I lie down on the floor, bring my knees up, and rotate them.

"Jesus, Andy, you got a PhD in counseling. People tell me all the time what a great help you are to them."

"Why they gave me a degree for *Ordinary Daylight* I don't know." This is what I know: nothing I can say helps. We accept what we can when we're finished with our temper tantrums but we know that blindness stinks, unless we listen to those irritating blindness organizations that keep yammering that being blind is no big deal. What are these idiots thinking? True, if you're born blind, it's altogether different. You know that you are complete, no matter what is missing. But I know very well what is missing because it was all there—the colors, the faces, the speed of travel and reading, the give and take. Blindness is devastating, mythic, mammoth, monstrous. Believing in karma, leaving it all up to some fucking higher power, being stalwart and positive and optimistic, finding the good hiding inside the bad, accepting blindness as a lesson, a test to overcome, feeling superior to the unblemished, the untested, seems as silly as optimism itself.

In our hotel room, Loie directs me to knobs and handles, to the bathroom door, the chair, sink, shower, and toilet. I follow her and run my hand along them, install a map of the space in my brain, and try not to be a klutz. "It's shocking how much you have to do for me wherever we go," I tell her. "I should be better at this." She disregards my whining. I say, "Just about everyone I ever met at the Seeing Eye bumps into nothing. They can hear the fucking chairs and sofas."

"You know that that's bullshit," she says, then: "I sometimes watch you and Gabriel making your way through town and realize that you're the bravest man I know."

What she may not know is that on my angry days, I want to mow people down. "Take that," I want to snarl as my dog and I plow through a group of sighted people, unaware that an important blind guy is making his royal way through town. It's a lot worse when I try it with a cane—tap tap. Tap tap. Here comes that blind guy. Without the dog, I am a traveling land mine. I can destroy furniture, unearth plants, knock pedestrians to the ground, dent my forehead, my shins and knees and shoulders. When I stop paying attention for one moment and no longer know where I am, I've learned to ask for help. "Where am I in relation to the pharmacy?" I ask, hoping that someone is nearby and listening.

"The pharmacy? It's way down there."

"Where?"

"There."

Cane or dog, I can't allow myself to be lost in thought. Did Gabriel stop at that damn blended curb? Which curb is coming up? If he ever forgets the three stone steps on my way to town, I will crack my skull. Being blind is exhausting. "I can't even imagine what it's like," Loie says. "If I were blind, I wouldn't ever leave the house. Or go to Poland."

4.

Buried deep in the genome of a Potok progenitor are the many genes responsible for a mutation known as retinitis pigmentosa, the prevalent heritable eye disease leading to blindness. In my case, there is no certain genetic antecedent, the one possibility anecdotal. My parents spoke of my grandmother Paulina, née Prokocimer, my father's mother, having had more lights on in her Bedzin home than any of the neighbors, and they suspected her of night blindness, the earliest troublesome feature of RP. And if so, mine was an inadvertent gift from my father who was asymptomatic, a gift I passed on to one of my two children, my daughter Sarah, and she to her two beautiful daughters, Anna and Rachel. Sharing this unwanted gift with the generations that follow me has produced remorse, guilt, rage, and sadness, all of which stick to me like barnacles, exacerbated now by being in the land where it probably began.

A few short years after our arrival in New York, I sat quietly in Herr Doktor's office as Herr Doktor Professor, recommended by one of my mother's new, rich customers, said in German, so quietly that my parents leaned far forward in their chairs, "Ach, this boy, he vill be blind," a prognosis never shared with me. During high school, I went often to the Hayden Planetarium to see the stars, the only stars I ever saw. Once, at Radio City Music Hall, I left my date to find the bathroom and, feeling my way back by touching each of the counted seatbacks, I never found my girlfriend again. At the beginning of the 1950s, a notice from the draft board demanded my presence at the Whitehall Induction Center in New York. I passed all the physical exams and was classified as 1A, fit for war. It took a couple of weeks for me to visualize myself in some ditch on the Korean peninsula in the middle of the black black night having my throat slit by anyone who could see at night. Embarrassed, I called the recruiters to tell them of my night blindness and trudged back to Whitehall where a doctor shone his ophthalmoscope into my eyes and yelled to his buddy, "Hey, have a look at this guy's eyes." A couple of them came over and peered into my face with their ophthalmoscopes. "See all that shit on his retina? It's retinitis pigmentosa." Apparently there was black gunk beginning to bury the pink photoreceptor cells. Their medical delight in seeing this on the retina of a live human being scared the shit out of me, but my 1A was changed to a 4F. I walked out into the street, relieved to be freed from an ugly battlefield death but understanding that the alternative destiny was not so hot either. Nevertheless, I chose architecture, then painting, still not suspecting the "inevitable blindness" that accompanied RP's description in any medical text.

In my late thirties, newly married to my second wife, Charlotte, we were driving back home from a chamber music concert at Dartmouth. As always after dark, Charlotte was at the wheel.

The night was cold and clear, the road home smooth. I was humming a lovely cello phrase from the first movement of the Schubert we had just heard and, staring at one of the bright rear lights of the car ahead of us, I watched it disappear. I shot up in my seat. When my gaze shifted a degree to left or right, the light returned. Terror struck, I managed to say, "I don't know what's happening."

"What?"

I shook my head violently, then hit my forehead with the palm of my hand.

"What are you doing?"

"Something terrible is happening to my eyes."

"What's happening? Should I pull over?"

Early the next morning, I called my ophthalmologist in New York. "No, Andy," she said, and took a deep breath. "It's not the dilation," she said. A few days earlier, I had spent half the day for my periodic check of the progression of the dread retinitis pigmentosa, which, thus far, had taken little other than night vision. In her office, my fingers played with a black and white Egyptian eye she had brought back from her world travels. She played the cello in a family quartet, the perfect woman, the perfect mother. After the dilation, going out into the sunlight was always painful, the streets blurred but, as usual, it all came to rights by morning. But not this time. Maybe the road back to normal was impeded by—what?—a dust particle, a sleepy neuron. "Andy," she repeated on the phone, "dear Andy, your eyes are back to normal, but it's a new normal."

"The new normal?" What was she talking about?

"It's the cones, the receptors in the center," she said.

"But I thought it was supposed to go from the outside in."

"Usually it does," she said, "but retinitis pigmentosa is unpredictable," then in a coarse whisper, "fucking unpredictable."

"I'm going to lose my central vision?" I heard her breathing but she said nothing. "The end of painting?"

"Andy," she said, "I've known you for a few years. You're strong. You have to stay strong. Promise me you'll paint as long as you can."

5.

I am the furthest from feeling like my father when making love or making art. The act of painting with oil on canvas began with the erotic, turned into playfulness, and only then got serious and dealt with the technical problems of balance, surface versus depth, interactions and interconnections of color, symmetries and asymmetries, and the demands imposed by the moment, with its immediate dictates on experience, history and culture, philosophy and rhetoric.

My affair with art began in this Poland, once my home, my safety, my childhood innocence, my first language, my earliest sense of landscapes that gave birth to my moods and passions. "You have always been a moody boy," I hear my mother's voice from way back. When I was cheerful, my nanny and I took a trolley to the spacious, airy park with a beautiful white castle on a lake, as well as Chopin's weeping willow tree. In my darker moods, we walked to the Saski Gardens, the somber, mysterious park where I first touched a horse chestnut. Elderly ladies sat on the benches along the path and, sliding their cold hands from the fur muffs on their laps, pointed out the fallen chestnuts. From the moment I touched the moist, shiny brown nut inside the shell, my heart raced and a new world stared at me. The green burrs were sometimes split by their long drop to the ground. More exciting still, I forced them open with my fingers, which slid inside to touch the smoothest, most delicious tissue, a bared cornucopia of unimagined delights. The radiance, sheen, and luster of the burnt umber nuts begged to be recreated, worshipped. Decades later, the oily pigments squeezed into shiny blobs on the palette gave me similar heart palpitations and my passion for art and sensuality was reborn.

In architecture school we labored at drafting tables, wielding T squares and slide rules; we wore khakis and proper shirts with rolled-up sleeves, a far cry from the life of alienation and despair, the one I, a hopeless romantic, wanted to inhabit. I still sometimes wonder if my pursuit of the latter required a compromise between fashion and art. Nevertheless, my idiotic need for agony and ecstasy was satisfied by the great Louis Kahn, the architect of the building where we worked, a great poet-artist, one side of his face seared by fire. Louis Kahn prowled the building under his magnificent tetrahedrons while Eugene Nalle, a shadowy poetic figure, a steel plate in his head from, I hoped, some daring event, lurked quietly about the drafting room, offering allusions and metaphors, and at times arcane symbols from unknown cultures for us poor slobs to interpret.

In color class, Josef Albers, the master of color and the square, spoke not only of art, but of his sensuous experiences as he roamed the streets of New Haven. "Ach, I am valking down—vot is de name of dat street?—und open de overcoat." We eagerly await the revelation. "Vot do I see? Inside de blue lining, I see a picture of—vot is de name of dat *schrecklich* building?—dere vere is de dinosaurs . . ." And we all wished we had an overcoat with a blue silk lining, at least, and also the sensitivity, the awareness of the extraordinary ordinary. Another day, Albers would report, "I cannot valk on de floor of dat building. De design—vot dey tink?—Islam arabesque? Up and down it goes. It is not for walking. It is to trip and fall like drunk." More than the theory behind his many homages to the square, he taught a careful mindfulness to the endlessly interesting configurations of the world through which we wandered.

I never thought of my origins then, not the horse chestnuts or the war's terrible effects on my family, dead or alive, or on me. The aim was to steer clear of it, to immerse myself in the non-material, imagined, created by me alone. When I quit architecture school to devote myself entirely to painting, I studied in Paris with the neo-cubist Andre Lhote, together with a bunch of Americans on the GI bill. After a day of painting, some of us spent long nights drinking Pernod or absinthe, trashing or defending our developing styles of angst-ridden expressionism or abstractions softened by Matisse-like sensibility or a neo-neo-cubism.

Only a few denied that painting was the expression of intangible ideas and experiences, that the subject of art emerged from the sheer act of making a painting. Some were searching for the sublime; some said that our canvases did not simply hold an image but an event, that the studio was a bullring, the act of painting a bullfight, a drama, a matter of life and death.

A year after Lhote, I signed up to work in the Beaux arts atelier of the neo-impressionist Maurice Brianchon, all of whose students painted Dufy-like boat scenes with colorful flags blowing in the breeze and neo-impressionist *dejeuners sur l'hcrbe* or *sur bateau* as well as tasty nudes. The students' wrists and elbows danced stylishly; their fanciful brushwork was charming and seductive, as they laid on delicacies, *mille feuilles,* and eclairs.

The Beaux arts experience did not feed me the meal I was searching for. The deeper understanding—that longed-for, authentic, profound communion with art and artists— arrived slowly, with the help of the Goya Black Paintings at the Prado and Giotto's frescoes in Assisi and Padua, with the still lives of Georges Braque and Hans Hoffman's color and structure, the depth and meaning of black in the work of Willem De Kooning, Robert Motherwell, and Franz Kline, who enabled me to disgorge what boiled inside, to eradicate the world of power and propaganda, the diurnal miasma of taste and fashion. Then, with the domestication that accompanied my move to a home in Vermont, my work settled into a gentler lyrical abstraction, as did the work of two of my admired painters of the time, Nicolas de Stael and the California painter Richard Diebenkorn.

But as color perception and detail slowly faded, I built very large sculptures that I painted in vivid colors. The blacks, the whites, the screaming hot colors in huge circles and tall columns looked magnificent when they were first exhibited in a wide open green landscape. I finished up my sighted art work with a series of assemblages: ten large boxes with epoxied, welded, or screwed-on gauges and pipes, electrical circuits, pumps and solenoids, atomic rejects, all painted with bright and sparkling marine paints, now rotting in the cellar of the Richardson Street house.

And then, in my early forties, as the center of my retina, the macula, was being cloaked by the black gunk of unabsorbed pigment, as I felt more and more raw and vulnerable, a non-entity, unmoored, empty, stateless, when straight lines had blown apart and colors had turned to mud, the good doctor of my mind gave me permission to stop.

Sitting on a rock at the highest point of my land, where a neighbor's cows sometimes grazed, a place where I had sat many times in the past to shake off a rage, some slight, some trivial infatuation, I now contemplated suicide. Could I? If so, how? Seated in this most silent, isolated place, I also imagined a ritual, a wake, a Kaddish, my work laid to rest in well-crafted hardwood crates, with dozens of good friends chanting and dancing in a circle, the bonfire burning higher than the treetops.

6.

I began training at St. Paul's Rehabilitation Center for Newly Blinded Adults, which became my residence for the next few months. There, I joined fifteen people who were also facing the end of their world as they knew it. Except for watching a blind person tapping his way along Fifty-Ninth Street, I'd had no contact with blind people, and was not eager to confront our mutual freakiness.

A guy calling himself a mobility instructor led me up the stairs to the men's sleeping quarters, a shabby conglomeration of bunks, the space as tight as that aboard some slovenly eighteenth-century sailing clipper. "Now," he said, "three steps forward, a right angle left, and the bathroom is straight ahead." He took my hand and led it to sink, toilet, and shower. I could have figured it out with my remaining eyesight but now I was in Atlantis, the mythic world of the blind.

The trainers taught us the proper use of a white cane, Braille, and something they called "techniques of daily living." Seeing too much, I spent most of every day blindfolded, preparing for what I knew was coming. For the first couple of days, the whole group sat together in a semicircle, no one daring to break the silence but, once we did, everyone was dying to tell his or her story. Within moments of a breakout story, everyone spoke at once. Having feared this nightmare, I was instead struck by a lightning bolt. I understood that I was with people who were in the same lifeboat as me, though we had little in common except for the blindness that now defined us. But that was more than enough. Like grunts in a platoon of draftees, we developed strong kinships—as befuddled cane travelers, numb-fingered scratchers of Braille, careful eaters of peas from forks, a band of children fighting the institutional hierarchical system of social workers and administrators. They became my community, so much so that in spite of being encouraged to go home for weekends, I chose to stay in our primitive accommodations, preferring them to the comfort of my bed, family, and friends.

Back home among the sighted, a new category, my friends wanted to touch my white cane and the exotic equipment, magnifiers of every conceivable kind, kits for sewing buttons, measuring cups and spoons, catalogues of talking levels and scales. But they were fascinated not only by my new widgets, but also by an unknown and alien world, introduced to them by one of their own. In fact, because I lived at the top of a long dirt road, a fifteen-minute walk to the village below, the cane turned out not to be all that useful and, because Charlotte was a very good cook, neither were the "techniques of daily living." In our kitchen, I didn't have to listen to burgers frying or to time a medium boiled egg with my newly sensitized ears or talking timer. So there I was again, not yet blind but not sighted either, belonging in neither world.

"Why don't you get a PhD?" my friend Gerry, the president of Goddard, the local college, asked.

"A PhD? In what?"

"I don't know," he said, "but you'll think of something." He could have suggested that I join the Merchant Marine and I would have done it.

I tried to give a shape to my life, a bell curve right side up or, turned around, sagging, or a pyramid, a circle, humdrum or exotic, driven off course by war, betrayals, and blindness. Could I do art history if I couldn't see the art? What about the history of music or of Europe in the twentieth century, both very appealing? Some blind people I knew chose counseling others going blind or those taking to the bottle, but I found the thought of spending the day in vain efforts to alter behavior seriously boring. Instead, I blew off the academic world and flew to London in pursuit of a woman who claimed that she could cure not only any old blindness, as one might expect from a quack, but, specifically, retinitis pigmentosa. I allowed Julia Owen, a pearshaped Austrian sadist, to cheerfully administer as many as fifteen bees daily to the back of my neck and alongside my ears. "Isn't this what we all do in a milder form when we pop multivitamins or serotonin reuptake inhibitors or get sloshed?" I asked Charlotte who flew to London with me.

"It doesn't usually include transatlantic airfare," she said or, as it turned out, a miserable six months, neck and cheeks bursting like overripe plums, the pain constant and without end.

When Julia Owen asked me and the dozen or so others she was abusing to write testimonials, we snapped to attention and, of course, we turned in neatly handwritten pages, mine illustrated with angelic bees in the margins.

"How could you write that garbage?" Charlotte asked when she visited during my fourth month.

My illustrated testimonial bought me another two months of torture, during which I continued to tape-record commentary on each day's events; thoughts about quackery, medicine, normalcy; and the fear of facing a life without eyesight. When I returned home, uncured and humiliated, I had the tapes transcribed and sent to the friend who first read me the *Telegraph* article, hoping for understanding, sympathy, and a few chuckles. She, then an editor for the *New York Times*, called the next day. "It's a book," she said. I joined an MFA writing program for one semester, then sent a chapter each month to an adjunct faculty member engaged in writing his own memoir, which helped produce my first book, *Ordinary Daylight*. It was well published, well reviewed, a life-changing event. Not only did the Julia Owen lunacy cure me of ever again seeking a cure for the incurable, but it led to a different kind of salvation, a new career.

4

A NOTE FROM MARTIN LUTHER

1.

According to British historian Tony Judt's *Post-War: A History of Europe Since 1945*, of the 126,000 Jews in pre-war Austria, some 4,500 returned after the war. In the Netherlands, of 140,000 Jews, 110,000 were deported and fewer than 5,000 returned. In France, 76,000 were deported and less than 3% survived. In Germany, 21,450 Jews survived out of a pre-war total of 600,000. And in Poland, 97.5% of the Jews were exterminated. Those who returned were not welcomed, but instead blamed for their own suffering; and worse, thousands were murdered by Poles. In Paris, where one returning Jew tried to reclaim his occupied apartment, a mob formed, chanting, "La France aux Francais."

I have never understood why there is so much hatred of Jews. When did all this begin? The religious scholar Reza Aslan writes that when Pontius Pilate ordered Jesus's crucifixion, he was absolved by Jesus himself, who was supposed to have told him that it was not he but the Jews who ordered the torture on the cross. According to Aslan, that moment— plus a horde of plutocrat Jews crying out that they had no king except Caesar—marked the beginning of anti-Semitism. Aslan does not explain why those folks chose Jesus and Christianity rather than another of the many available sects, except to conjecture that "the resurrection was the deciding factor," staged or not. It was missing from the myths of other sects, and thus the Jesus sect has survived for two millennia so far and is as violent a sect as any other.

On each side of the beginning of the Christian era, every messianic group was allowed to ply its trade until it failed to conform in some way to the scriptures and prophecies; these sacred texts, thought to be divinely inspired, were blindly accepted.

I too am awed by the unseen, unheard, unsmelled, and unfelt, the reality of space-time, quantum mechanics, quarks and gluons—universal truths that do not ask for obeisance, fealty, or prayer. In my view, imagination can be better used in the creation of art than in populating a heaven and hell with gods and goddesses, angels and devils.

But in the realm of hope and faith, anything is possible. Faith and reason do live side by side, like unicorns and goats, but once the ancestral fears of lightning and thunder, earthquakes and floods vanished, we were left with the prospect of a heavenless oblivion, with only our fellow human beings to fear.

One friend sent me on an intellectual expedition into theodicy, a justification of the existence of an omnipotent, omniscient God in a world replete with natural disasters, slaughter, and human evil; but the notion of theodicy and its concomitant belief in a mystical force running the whole show is interesting only to believers.

I don't know how to tolerate, for instance, the wish to kill or die on behalf of one trumped-up messiah or another, the scramble for ever-odder self-help schemes preventing a critical look into the real causes of the political hold on inequity and the violence that is inequity's certain consequence.

At the time of Christ in Palestine, it seems that everyone was hell-bent on finding the Kingdom of God, zealot seekers appearing principally during reigns of immorality, not unlike our own time, especially in America, where fundamentalists chase after angels, gurus, and shamans. The religious scholar Reza Aslan writes that when Pontius Pilate ordered Jesus's crucifixion, he was absolved by Jesus himself who was supposed to have said that it was the Jews who ordered his crucifixion and therefore Pontius Pilate had nothing to feel guilty about. That moment, plus a horde of the plutocrat Jews of the time crying out that they had no king except Caesar, according to Aslan, marked the beginning of anti-Semitism. He does not explain why those folks chose Jesus and Christianity rather than another of the many available sects, except to conjecture that "the resurrection was the deciding factor," staged or not. It was missing from the myths of other sects, and thus the Jesus sect has survived for two millennia so far and is as violent a sect as any other.

Four centuries after it was decided to restart the calendar at zero and the Romans were fully Christianized, Christian literature began to display extreme hostility toward Jews. The accusation of deicide that is still with us, especially in Poland, led to the burning of synagogues and the killing of Jews.

Appearing at this time was the revered theologian John Chrysostom, now Saint John Chrysostom. He preached Eight Homilies Against the Jews, "the pitiful and miserable Jews, brute animals concerned only with food and lust, although such beasts are not fit for work, they are fit for killing." Christ himself was supposed to have said: "But as for my enemies who did not want me to be king over them, bring them here and slay them."

In Europe during the Middle Ages a full-scale persecution of Jews gained steam. Libels, expulsions, forced conversions, and murders became the standard. Between 1400 and 1600 Western Europe was more or less "a world free of Jews." Banished from most countries, and existing only in the tiniest numbers through special exemptions, actual Jews were hardly ever seen. But this was the time of Christian Europe's conviction that it was becoming too Jewish. During this period of cultural change and doctrinal and political disputes, adversaries of Christianity had to be extinguished.

Martin Luther brought this rhetoric to a fever pitch. In 1523 he accused the Roman Church of becoming "more 'Jewish' than the Jews," and as he grew older he tried to convince his contemporaries that "so thoroughly hopeless, mean, poisonous, and bedeviled a thing are the Jews that for 1400 years they have been, and continue to be, our plague, pestilence, and all that is our misfortune." In 1543 Luther published *On the Jews and Their Lies*, in which he wrote that "the Jews are venomous beasts, vipers, disgusting scum, devils incarnate, a base, whoring people, no people of God. . . . Set their synagogues and schools on fire, destroy their prayer books, forbid their rabbis to preach, raze their homes, confiscate their property and money. They should be shown no mercy or kindness, afforded no legal protection, and these poisonous envenomed worms should be drafted into forced labor or expelled for all time." He provided detailed recommendations for a pogrom against them, calling for their permanent oppression and expulsion, writing, "Their private houses must be destroyed and devastated, they could be lodged in stables. If this avails nothing, we will be compelled to expel them like dogs in order not to expose ourselves to incurring divine wrath and eternal damnation from the Jews and their lies." At one point Luther wrote, "We are at fault in not slaying them," a passage that may be termed "the first work of modern anti-Semitism, and a giant step forward on the road to the Holocaust."

In the Germany of the 1930s and '40s, the only morality was fidelity to race, making any non-racist attitude such as mercy to the weak a destructive Jewish idea. According to this German racist philosophy, reason over impulse drew the races away from the natural human struggle and resulted in the decimation of the species. Jews were weak, cowardly, and gutless. Reciprocity, peacefulness, and ethical considerations were considered poisonous Jewish ideas, and yet, at the same time, these "philosophical Jews" were accused of a fierce hunger for world domination.

The European Jews who survived the Holocaust were given an inhabited land in middle eastern Asia by munificent colonialist Europeans used to remaking boundaries, not so much as reparations to a victimized people as for geopolitical reasons. Why did they choose Palestine rather than, say, Germany as the Jewish homeland? Why not Germany or at least a part of it? How about Bavaria or the Rhine Valley, with maybe the Ruhr Valley thrown in? That would certainly have provided enough land for the eight million Jews who now inhabit Palestine. Perhaps not all but many people in the world would have understood if a few million German perpetrators were forced to give up their land. Those Germans could have squeezed into what was left in Germany or shipped to, say, Madagascar. So why Palestine, as much the homeland to those strange Arabs who lived there as far back as the Jews, who, like them, felt a cockamamy God-given right to the place.

It may be naïve to express a deep emotion regarding Israeli attitudes toward Palestinians but it's almost impossible for me to understand why the beneficiaries of this donation, the Jews in Israel, have no problem uprooting others and are capable of egregious disregard for human life and dignity. Shouldn't one expect Jews, after all they've been through, to be morally superior? It seems that no amount of victimhood, no matter how unspeakably ghastly, prevents victims from becoming oppressors when the chance arises. Now that there is a Jewish homeland, and nationhood provides, for some, a sense of belonging, it also allows, even assures, the worst components of national behavior: pridefulness, pitilessness, and exclusiveness. Every nation state is capable of indulging in uncivilized ways, surrounded by angry neighbors or not. Even though Israel will never be my home, as a Jew I can't escape feeling a certain sense of pride as well as feeling implicated in the heartless decimation of Palestinians.

When, in the early 1960s, I flew from Greece, where my then-wife Joan, my two little kids, and I were living, to meet my mother in Israel, both she and I felt enormous pride, both of our hearts racing with the feeling that this might be the first and only place where we can be safe as Jews. "Can you believe it," my mother asked me, "that Jewish people are farming their own land and driving the trains?" Even though I did not feel unsafe in Greece or in America, my entire body felt different in Israel, unburdened of the fear of hatred or expulsion. But after nearly a week in Israel, I yearned to fly back to Greece, the philosophical and art home, the one where my mind felt free.

But where in the worldview called Judaism do atheists like me belong? If religion is the glue that has held Jews together against all odds for millennia, then what replaces that glue for people like me who do not obey any list of commandments, instructions, or prophecies; no prescriptions from an angry Old Testament God or from the milder Christian one? Proclaiming my Jewishness has nothing at all to do with religious beliefs, nor is it based on the refusal to leave a sinking ship, or the fear of abandoning others like me who have been the despised scapegoats of the world. Rather, it's the pride that has grown with every unhappy visit to Poland, the pride of having survived in spite of them.

In his book *Anti-Judaism*, David Nirenberg considers the intellectual history of Western civilization in Christian and post-Christian thought, the role of anti-Judaism being a central theological and political idea. According to Nirenberg, the negative view of Judaism established in the earliest Christian polemics became a common tool in many different intellectual efforts to understand the world and to denounce opposing understandings. Jews were considered guilty of the stubborn adherence to flesh, and were therefore enemies of the spirit and of God; they were accused of enticing Christians to believe in law instead of love, the letter instead of the spirit, the material world instead of the soul. Nirenberg shows that many of the important conceptual and aesthetic developments from Saint John to Saint Augustine to Muhammad, from Shakespeare to Luther to Hegel, depended on denigrating Jews. For thousands of years the patterns of anti-Judaism have evolved to provide great thinkers and ordinary citizens with ways to make sense of their world. In the modern period, revolutionaries and counter-revolutionaries continued to use "the Jewish problem" as something to be overcome. "How could that tiny minority convincingly come to represent for so many the evolving evils of the capitalist world order?" Nirenberg asks.

And why is this tiny minority treated as though it was responsible for the evils of Stalinism? Was it the convenient myth in Eastern Europe of a Judeo-Bolshevik alliance? Many intellectuals of the left hoped for years that something was out there to reduce the inequity, the disgraces of capitalism. They proved to be wrong, but a hope lingers and it is the hope of decent people alike, Jews and non-Jews. And yet in Poland and every other eastern European nation, when Jews were no longer slaughtered just because they were Jews, they were slaughtered for being Communists.

It was not only the caricatures of ugly misshapen Jews

from Julius Streicher's *Der Stürmer* tabloid, which had a circulation of 480,000 German readers, but the belief that money was the motivating force in the Jewish psyche. Aside from the fact that a huge majority of European Jews were poor, the few who did amass great fortunes did so in similar ways to Christian robber barons. It is probably impossible for anyone to get filthy rich without filthy deeds, without stepping over dead bodies, without lying and cheating, without destroying others.

In Claude Lanzmann's monumental film *Shoah*, one of the two surviving fighters from the Warsaw Ghetto Uprising, then living in Israel, says, "If anyone opened me up and kissed my heart, they would be poisoned." Even though I have not earned the right to feel that kind of hatred, I understand it, unwilling and unable to ever erase thoughts from my mind of so many ordinary German men causing such persistent, relentless agony.

For me the most unforgettable scene in the film is of a boy, I think Janek by name, now a young man, who sits in front of a lineup of Poles, the church whose services they just left behind them, screaming at Lanzmann that they have always loved Jews. The look on Janek's face, over whose head they are shouting, is one of shame, empathetic shame, his innate morality bringing a blush to his face, his sweetness almost unable to bear the hypocrisy. Thus unforgiving hatred and rage contrasts with the shame—empathetic shame at best—of those Poles who deny the poisonous nature of their Jew hatred.

Once born into a tribe or a nation, we belong. We appear and are defined as Americans, Poles, Jews, Muslims, or Christians. Being born in any country is a matter of chance. But what does belonging to a tribe of Germans, Poles, Americans, or Israelis mean? A strong ambivalence has always existed within me, a wrestling match between a deep desire to belong and the equally powerful need to remain an outsider. It's lonely not to belong, but then, what can I belong to without reservation or shame?

They say that only Catholic Poles are true owners of Polish land. Jews, as the lady in Warsaw told me years ago, are visitors, and visitors exist at the whim of the owner. Every country lives with its own mythology, based on chosen morsels of history, true or imagined. But the North American nineteenth-century expansion west did not make Americans frontiers people; that tendency is not an inherited trait. Gun ownership among pioneers doesn't translate into the joy of shooting folks with guns today. Poland has had a much longer history, yet only some inhabitants feel they have the right to claim to be "ethnic Poles." This unhappy territory has been inhabited by Scythian, Celtic, Germanic, Baltic, and Slavic tribes. Not a Jew among them until a thousand years ago. Still visitors? You bet. A thousand years? The blink of an eye. It depends on who is counting. Though at times over the centuries secular authorities have tried to moderate violence toward Jews in order to sustain the economy, the Roman Catholic Church pushed hard for their exclusion, considering them a despised sect, a danger to the church. Morality never entered the picture.

5

13 STRADOMSKA STREET

1.

After breakfast on our second morning in Krakow, Loie and I set out to see the apartment house on Stradomska Street, the reason we are here. We negotiate the narrow, winding, icy Kazimierz streets and, in spite of the horrible weather, Loie points out some of the small tourist attractions. "There's one called Theta Café," she says, and snaps a photo for her New Age West Coast friend for whom theta waves lead to health and happiness. I'm freezing but it's never too cold for the sudden appearance of Loie's iPhone. "Oh my God, Andy," she says a few minutes later as I stomp the pavement in my city shoes, "it's a restaurant with a large picture of Che Guevara in the window"—an image soon to be mailed to my idealistic grandson Nickie. We pass groups of Israeli high school students gathered at the entrances of restored synagogues, the kids equipped with yarmulkes and backpacks, singing folk tunes and clapping.

We emerge on a wide busy street, Stradomska Street, humming with electric trams, speeding traffic, people huddled in their winter coats jumping over snowbanks and, like us, skidding on the treacherous ice. But something grips me, something beyond the daily comedy of slipping and jumping, beyond traffic or the conversations in the street or inside the shops or trolley cars. It is the feeling of a hovering blanket of danger, of alien nationhood, toxic and impenetrable to people like me.

"There's a Number Thirteen here but it's just an entrance to a shabby courtyard," Loie reports. "This can't be it," she says, but nevertheless we step into a long, narrow forlorn looking area. "Andy," she says, "I don't know how to tell you this but it doesn't look inhabited."

"Not inhabited?"

"Electric wires are hanging from the windows, paint is peeling, shutters are falling apart."

My stomach begins to ache. "We came for this?"

"At the far end, I see an Italian restaurant," Loie says. "Giuseppi's or Botticelli's or some damn name. It's an old sign and I can't make it out."

"Are there people?"

She says nothing for a moment.

"Waiters?"

"No, but I do see tables and chairs, some bottles in the window. Cars parked near the entrance, but no people."

"It's supposed to be an apartment house," I murmur. "My grandmother couldn't have lived here." Loie puts her arm through mine. What is with me? Instead of feeling solace, I'd like to take the next plane out of here, to forget we ever came.

"What can I tell you?" Loie says.

"Maybe before the war . . ." I begin.

"Maybe if there were pots of flowers on the balconies," she says.

"Balconies? There are balconies?"

"And shutters," she says, "but they're broken, off their hinges. If it were an Italian slum, they'd have spruced it up. There would be something gay about it."

68

"Not that we ever imagined a little pied-à-terre in Krakow," I muse in spite of a growing awareness of the emptiness of this quixotic journey. "What a thought! How could this piece of shit be worth the kind of money Artur predicted?"

Totally dejected, we find a little café not far from Number Thirteen. "Many of the buildings on Stradomska Street have huge nets tightly cinched around their facades," Loie reports.

"It's to keep the crumbling stone from crushing passersby."

"Why are they crumbling?"

"The giant Lenin Steel Works, Nowa Huta, spewed particulates into the atmosphere, destroying many beautiful Medieval and Renaissance buildings and churches. The last time I was here, people walked around pressing handkerchiefs to their mouths and noses."

"You know, Andy," Loie says, "maybe the condition of the property doesn't matter. The location has to count for something. The street itself is central and wide," she says, "plenty of shops and a lot of traffic." We sip our coffees in silence for a while, our thinking now beginning to concentrate on location. After all, the property, though a tenement, is only a stone's throw from Wawel Castle, the gem of this city, the place where kings and queens of Poland lived. We ponder the implications of being owners of a Dickensian hovel and begin to walk up the long hill to the castle itself, a stupendous fortified complex of buildings begun by Casimir the Great in the fourteenth century on a site that has been populated since the Paleolithic Age. In one of its rooms hangs a Leonardo da Vinci oil on wood from 1489 called *Lady with an Ermine*. I hang on to Loie's elbow as we walk through the galleries. She's impressed but neither of us have the stamina to stay inside for long.

In October 1939, following the German invasion of

Poland, Hans Frank was named governor-general of all Poland and took up residence inside the castle. It has been said that he loved the Leonardo lady, as he did all of Beethoven. In one of the royal staterooms, on December 16, 1941, Hans Frank announced to his senior officials the approaching annihilation of the Jews. "What should we do with the Jews?" he asked. "We were told in Berlin, 'Why all this bother? We can do nothing with them either in Ostland or in the Reichskommissariat. So liquidate them.' Gentlemen, I must ask you to rid yourself of all feelings of pity. We must annihilate the Jews wherever we find them and whenever it is possible."

And so it went. Any European, especially a German, could have uttered those words, words not as shocking or distasteful as they might have been, if not for their religious and civic legitimization and long historical precedent.

From a bench on Wawal Hill overlooking the great Vistula River, I sit gloomily imagining Jews bound for Auschwitz being pushed into boats and trains, whipped, struck with rifle butts. "I wish you could see the view from here," Loie says. "It's majestic."

We walk down from Wawel Hill on this historic blood-soaked land, a ground zero of human evil, which some say can be a product of thoughtlessness; it can be banal, a concept pushed by Hannah Arendt in her coverage of the 1962 Eichmann trial in Jerusalem. She formulated the dangerous and wrong-headed idea that Adolf Eichmann's role in the murder of millions of Jews was the work of a clown rather than a monster, stating that, aside from his desire to improve his career, he simply followed orders and showed no anti-Semitism and was thus wrongly tried and hung. Somehow, she missed a large body of evidence that Eichmann boasted of his evil convictions. Evil can be banal, but just because so many humans are capable of its perpetration does not excuse its usage. Hannah Arendt's tendentious thinking regarding Jewish prominence as bourgeois capitalists allowed her to believe that Jews were partly responsible for their annihilation.

No matter the excuse, evil is an available human choice. For the poet W. H. Auden, evil is potential in everyone. In his poem "Herman Melville," Auden wrote: "Evil is unspectacular and always human / And shares our bed and eats at our own table." The philosopher and mystic Simone Weil (a convert from Judaism to Christianity), wrote, "Imaginary evil is romantic and varied; real evil is gloomy, monotonous, barren, boring."

When, the next day, I tell Artur about our dismay at the condition of Thirteen Stradomska, he seems surprised by my concern. "Once it is recovered, don't you have to sell it?" I ask him.

"Yes, of course," he says.

"Why would anyone want to buy such a place?"

"There is always someone," he tells me. I presume that a buyer would tear the dump down and build a handsome apartment building, but even though I loved living in cities such as New York and Paris, a handsome little apartment house on Stradomska Street, with trams, cars, and trucks whizzing by, neighboring buildings falling apart, the shops dingy and unpleasant, would never be my choice of location. "But Andrew," says Artur Bobrowski, "you must f-f-forget your taste and think of this as money in the b-b-bank. Remember that all of this is about a nephew of your grandmother's," he says. "This Edward Prokocimer in 1946 told the court that all the other inheritors of this property, your father and your uncle Stanislaw, were dead."

"This is so hard to believe," I say quietly.

"Not only that," says Artur, "but he stated that his own brother, B-B-Bruno, who survived the war in Paris, was also dead.

The substance and reality of betrayal has haunted me all

my life, and the news of another family betrayal brings old ones back to center stage. I sip my vodka and wonder about memory itself, often cast in stone, impregnable, encased in a thick-walled culvert protecting it from change. "When Edward died," Artur goes on, "he deeded the property to his son, Miron, who lives in Israel. We will recover it from Miron," he says.

"Why would Miron listen to a Polish judge's orders?" I ask. "Can't he simply dismiss the whole thing?" I entertain an image of a Polish posse riding through the Zin Valey in the Negev. "I am going to sue a relative," I say quietly to Loie.

"For money that is legally yours," Loie says sweetly.

Artur thinks for a minute. "No one wants to give away half of his fortune, so he might fight the court, which would only prolong the process. Then, not only will he lose the property but he will be forced to pay all the court fees." Artur has made his fortune doing precisely this kind of work for survivors now scattered all over the world. "In law school," he tells us, "I concentrated my studies on Polish law of 1946 and so I am equipped to challenge wrongful inheritance that the Polish court of the time permitted." He then reaches into his briefcase and pulls out a pack of papers for me to study, much of it the same genealogy of the family since 1830 that he described to me in Vermont; but before we go to court, he tells me, I need to be completely familiar with the names and, when known, the means and place of their wartime murders.

He reads aloud and it is as if I am hearing it for the first time. A stranger in my life and half my age, Artur reminds me that my father had a brother and sister whose existence had been totally unknown to me. My father's brother, my uncle Szymon, was transported by the Russians to a labor camp in Gorky where he died from tuberculosis that he contracted in the camp. And then there was my aunt, Aunt

Maryla, who, probably together with her son (likely my age at the time) and perhaps her mother, my grandmother Paulina, were dragged from a comfortable assimilated life and forced into the Bedzin Ghetto, then transported to Auschwitz to be murdered by ordinary German men, probably with the help of a Ukrainian or two, who were probably identified as Jews by Polish neighbors eager to occupy their houses. Artur's papers documented only broad details. But how could it have happened except like this? My aunt and cousin and my beloved grandmother were taken to the "showers," gassed with hundreds of other Jews, then reduced to ashes in a crematorium manufactured by a German corporation. I wonder if Paulina, at her age, had the strength to climb on other bodies, if the eleven-year-old cousin screamed at the bottom of the pile, or if Maryla held them both in her arms. My grandmother Paulina must have been brutalized by filthy alien hands on her body, selecting her, grabbing her, yanking, battering, pushing her into pits or showers or filthy bunks teeming with suffering humanity. I wonder if my grandmother's white hair was used to stuff some Berliner's mattress, if the gold fillings in her teeth were yanked out, if she prayed or if her God was already dead to her. I took it for granted that everyone in my family was murdered by Germans or Russians, Ukrainians or Poles, but the difference between knowing the general and knowing the particular is immense.

2.

Until I owned a house and land in Vermont, I had never felt at home, never felt I belonged anywhere. With that house came a joyous feeling of home until, one day, I remembered that, like my parents in Poland, I was merely a visitor in someone else's land. I wondered how my few surviving relatives felt about their displacement, then acculturation to a new country, surrounded by a new language, new landscapes.

My cousin Anna has lived in Gothenburg, a large city on the west coast of Sweden, since 1969. Also descended from that Potok patriarch born in the 1830s, Joachim David, she traces her lineage to his second marriage while I trace mine to his first. Not only were there eight surviving children from each of the two marriages, but there is some evidence that the inexhaustible Joachim married one more time, though no recorded births from that union have yet been found. Anna and I are both refugees but our experiences have been vastly different. She and her parents were forced to leave Warsaw because of the mass expulsion of Jews, accused by the government of being a Fifth Column, saboteurs and conspirators. The Gomulka government fabricated a narrative for the war years, claiming that, once again, those crafty Jews were spreading ugly rumors about Polish Jew hatred. Thus the ruling party rewrote World War II history, censoring all references to Poles who sent Jews to the death camps or helped with deportations or were simply silent bystanders. The new formulation declared that everyone was sent to extermination camps, especially Poles. Having established this revisionist history, Gomulka forced Jews out of government, academy, and business.

I was thirty-seven at the time, recently married to Charlotte, my political self engaged with American cities burning, the King and Kennedy assassinations, and the violence unleashed by Chicago Mayor Richard Daley at the 1968 Democratic Convention. I was totally ignorant about the expulsions of Jews from Poland.

"Of course it was different for me to be expatriated when I was twenty-three than for you at the age of eight," Anna tells me. In Sweden, where she has now lived for forty-five years, Anna still feels that she does not belong, not there in Gothenburg, not back in Warsaw, not any-where. Anna's father was a physician, her mother a school nurse and, like many others, they fled east at the outbreak of the war, ending up in a Soviet camp, where they were put to work in a military hospital. Like my London cousin Anita, when the war was over Anna and her parents went back to Poland. Though she had not experienced the war, she grew up in the midst of Warsaw rubble, the city destroyed by Germans and Russians. "Poland was my home. I had many friends and a language," Anna tells me, and I imagine her as a child buying a loaf of bread from the neighborhood bakery, helped by the shopkeeper who asks about her parents and puts the change into her little fists. Anna skips home, maybe munching an end of the loaf, stops at the curb, then crosses the street. A few years later, she sits at a café with a few girlfriends, telling each other stories of how their mothers came out of the bedroom rosy pink and smiling, and how their fathers grumbled as they read the day's newspaper. Then Warsaw University, a crush on a boy on the nearby bench, her first cigarette, the swal-low of vodka. "In Sweden I started a new part in my life. What to do? Learn a new language. My father started to work as an anesthetist in a little town not far from Gothen-burg. I studied Slavic languages at the university in Uppsala but, instead of teaching, I took a job with Volvo. Because of my language skills, I did a lot of work in Poland and all over the Soviet Union."

No matter the circumstances, childhoods are simply childhoods, one lived in war, another in peace. "It's like chil-dren who are born blind," I tell her, "and consider them-selves whole, entire, until they learn that others have a sense that they lack."

"Though I've been married to a Swede for many years," Anna says, "I have never felt at home in Sweden. I feel more and more like a stranger. To go back to Poland? Maybe, I don't know. Even though the reason why I had to leave Poland was that I am Jewish, at the time I did not think about it much. We never celebrated any Jewish holidays. I know nothing about Judaism." Anna speaks Swedish, English, and Russian, but she thinks and dreams in Polish. "I lost contact with most of my school friends. It was very strange to see Warsaw after so many years. When I walked all over the city, I realized that it was no longer my city. I panicked when I realized that I didn't belong there, and if not there, then nowhere."

My London Anita also feels that she does not belong anywhere. "Certainly not as a Jew," she says, "but I'm afraid not really as an English woman either." I'm surprised because she seems so very English, her language the Queen's English, her ease and comfort among the natives akin to mine in America.

The great Polish poet Czeslaw Milosz wrote, "A loss of harmony with the surrounding space, the inability to feel at home in the world, so oppressive to an expatriate, a refugee, an immigrant, paradoxically integrates him in contemporary society and makes him, if he is an artist, understood by all. Even more, to express the existential situation of modern man, one must live in exile of some sort."

6

PATRIMONY

1.

Memories of getting out of Poland remain skeletal, abridged by intervening time, necessarily incomplete. None of the adult participants are alive, though even when they were, talk of the past was strictly limited. But now that I'm here again walking the streets of this unwelcoming land, the frustration of unrecovered memory drives me crazy. Not only are records destroyed, but entire parts of the country, including large thriving cities, once in Poland, are now no longer so. Vilnius, Wilno in Polish, is now in Lithuania, while others, like Lwow, are part of Ukraine.

In mid-September 1939, the skies already darkened by German airplanes, and vast parts of the country flattened by tanks, I stood on the sidewalk in front of our Warsaw apartment house, hugged and kissed good-bye by tearful aunts, uncles, cousins, and grandparents. What did I know? My heart might have been beating fast, curious and eager to begin a new adventure. I thought that I was about to ride in Max's sky blue Packard with its gorgeous silver hubcaps on red and white wheels, a treat, war or no war, but my father took me by the hand and walked me over to the Citroen van which, in peacetime, had delivered fur coats to Apfelbaum's customers. Uncle Max's chauffeur, Twardowski, drove my aunt Zosia, her six-year-old daughter Anita, Anita's governess Pani Potocka, my father, and me. My mother, along with an aunt and uncle I hardly knew, rode in the Packard with Max at the wheel. "Where are we going?" I asked my father who sat next to me in the Citroen.

"Romania," he said. I think I saw fear on all the grown-ups' faces. How could they not have been afraid? Afraid that we *were* leaving too late, afraid that the cars would break down, afraid of bombs. It was a precarious time to leave, nearly two weeks since the first day of the war, and early in the morning the streets were fairly empty. On Marszalkowska, Twardowski ran inside the Apfelbaum salon and came back with many fur coats, which he piled up in the back of the van. I begged Twardowski to drive first to Wieliszew to pick up my new bicycle and was told that we didn't have time. I recited favorite poems, such as "Lokomotywa," about a huge locomotive chugging and steaming in the station before pulling its hundreds of cars through the countryside. A little way out of town, the roads were jammed, horns honking, people yelling and cursing. Our two cars drove south toward Romania until, in the city of Lublin, we were forced by blitzkrieg armies, one from the west, another from the east, to turn back; we skirted Warsaw and headed toward Lithuania. The road was packed with people fleeing in cars, trucks, horse-drawn wagons, bicycles, and on foot.

On the second day, they had to leave the beautiful Packard with Twardowski, who said he would return it when we came back after the war. Anita's governess, Pani Potocka, said that the Packard used too much gasoline, and so the four who rode in the Packard crowded into the Citroen van, which Max drove north, the direction determined not by plan but by changing circumstances.

On August 23 the German-Soviet Nonaggression Pact had been signed, and the two barbaric states planned to divide Poland, Romania, Latvia, Lithuania, Estonia, and Finland into one camp or the other. Until that date, the rational decision was to go east, as far from the Germans as possible, even though the Soviet Union, allied for the moment with Western powers, was hardly a safe destination for Jews. Still, it was the only destination that made sense at the time, and thus it was taken by much of my family, including my uncle Stash, London Anita and Swedish Anna's parents, and my Australian cousin Jurek and his family.

Lithuania was not exactly a haven for Jews either, but we in the Citroen made it to safety, while the ones who chose to drive east ended up in Soviet labor camps, where all but my father's brother Szymon survived.

My cousin Jurek, eleven years older than I, was nineteen when the war began. His father, the Izaak who made the gift of a stained glass window to a Krakow synagogue, was my grandfather Solomon's brother.

Jurek and his family lived in Krakow, managed a timber business, and owned a farm miles away where they spent every summer tending cows and horses; they loved being away from the city. "My parents left in the car," Jurek told me years ago. "I was on horseback, others in horse-drawn carts and horses, all headed toward the Romanian border. In Lwow, I spotted my father getting off a tram. This is what happens during war. By accident I found my family." In the middle of one night in 1940, a Russian soldier banged on the door of the flat they lived in, ordered them to pack one suitcase each, and put them into a cattle car bound for Siberia. There was no food or water. So each time the train stopped at a station, everyone ran to buy boiled water, almost undrinkable except for those who brought tea with them. They walked twenty-five kilometers from the railroad station through the rugged Ural Mountains and moved into one of the thatched huts, three or four families in each, some eight hundred people in all. From five in the morning until seven at night, they chopped down trees, sawed them into logs, and burned the branches, the ashes becoming the charcoal needed to make steel for the Russian war effort. They had to stack four cubic meters of wood in order to get the daily ration of four hundred grams of black, heavy, wet bread, plus soup in the morning and again at night. "It was very cold," Jurek said, "and we had to dig graves nearly every day for those who died from exhaustion, malnutrition, illness, or accidents." They lived like this for three years; then in 1942 the British and Americans made a deal to free 100,000 Polish prisoners of the millions in captivity.

Here their story parallels my uncle Stash's, who was freed to leave his labor camp near the Finnish border. Not knowing about each other's camp survival, they all found their way south, wherever that was and whatever the means, to thaw from the Russian winters. Jurek and his brother joined the Polish army in Persia where the Poles made him drop his pants to check for Jewishness, the Poles, of course, not wanting Jews to pollute their army. Jurek's mother found a priest to swear that her son was Catholic in spite of his circumcision. They passed through Tashkent, Tehran, Iraq, Karachi, and Mombasa in Kenya, to East Africa, Uganda, Tanganyika, and eventually to Egypt, where Jurek stayed for two years as a provisions officer for the Polish army. Also in the Polish army under British command, Stash fought in the Allied invasion of Italy, surviving some of the fiercest battles of the war. Both he and Jurek then settled in London, Stash for the rest of his life, Jurek until 1949 when he sailed on a cargo ship to Australia. "The war years were very very bad, but when I think back on it now, it doesn't seem so bad. We survived, the chance to do so a thousand times greater in Russia than under German occupation."

I don't know how Jurek's, Stash's, or London Anita's family escaped being murdered. Jurek and Stash were young men, and young men of fighting age were a potential danger, but then the slaughter included women and children for no other reason than their Jewishness. When the German offensive against the Soviet Union stalled in December 1941, everything changed in Germany's plans regarding the sub-human Slavs and non-human Jews. A German victory would have allowed for their deportation. Since the attack on the Soviet Union, the Germans were achieving their goal of ridding the world of Jews by means of mass shooting. Toward the end of 1941, a million Jews in western and central Soviet Union had already been murdered. Now the Germans had to figure out how to kill the remaining Jews. The game had changed. In the ghettos of Poland, tens of thousand of Jews had died of disease and malnutrition, but two million Jews were still alive in western and central Poland. How would these people be killed? Two million Soviet citizens had already died in the German starvation camps, and now the survivors as well as a million young men in the Soviet army were also persuaded to kill Soviet Jews.

Thus the despised Slavs were used to slaughter the more despised Jews. It is a wonder that Stash, Jurek and family, London Anita and her parents survived the Jew killers from Estonia, Belarus, Lithuania, Latvia, and Ukraine, many of whom were then used to help with the extermination of the Jews in death camps.

Jurek's wife, Liane, tells me that in 2006, when they were on a cruise from Copenhagen to St. Petersburg, they spent a day in Gdynia, and Jurek refused to go ashore. Neither Stash nor Jurek ever set foot in Poland again.

2.

How to recapture the mood in our car, now headed for the Lithuanian border? What was I even capable of thinking? Terror obliterates everything. Maybe I tried to think of horse chestnuts in the Saski Gardens, or hum a song about Jarek buying a lamb bone at the village market or the sorry national anthem. I must have wanted Max to drive fast, to drive straight ahead, make no more turns. I must have understood that we didn't want to die, and yet I had never buried a rabbit or a bird so what did I know about death? In some Polish children's book, there must have been mention of heaven. My mother kept saying, *"Borze, Borze,"* God, God. She was asking for help from someone I didn't know about, someone she turned to when the humans around her were mean or angry or didn't pay attention. I might have remembered once springing up in the middle of the night, already night-blind, walking into doorjambs or toys on the floor. Barefoot and cold, I walked into the dining room where the nursemaid was polishing the silver. I touched her and cried. I said I was afraid. She didn't turn toward me. She said nothing. I ran back to my room and buried my head under the pillows.

In the front seat of the car, Max was yelling at other cars and farm trucks and horse-drawn carts, while my mother who sat next to him tried to calm him, always her job. Next to me, my father's head was in his hands. He said nothing but then he never said much. Would we win or would we lose? What would happen if we lost? "Go, go, go," I thought, and then the sky began to hum louder and louder until the planes were nearly above us and the van jerked to a stop. Max yelled to get out and we jumped into the ditch. Clumps of earth exploded, strafing bullets whizzed by, blowing earth and grass flat. My ears filled with the rattling of bullets, voices screaming, horses neighing. I buried my face in the mud and stones and garbage until the airplanes droned off to other targets and we ran back to the Citroen. Car doors slammed shut. People screamed. Dead or mutilated horses were dragged into the ditches. In school, we'd made cardboard gas masks, laughing at how silly we all looked. Now I felt alone, and touched the metal of the inside of the car, slid my hand over its curves and bumps. It was freezing cold and I lay my cheek on the icy metal.

When the red and white striped barrier of the border crossing appeared, the mood inside the van changed. Everyone stirred. We were close to getting out. One by one, border guards examined the cars. Some were allowed through, some pushed to the side. Our van inched ahead, hardly moving. There were five or ten cars in front of us. Polish soldiers hobbled past our van and threw their rifles into a growing pile before getting in line to walk across the border. Two Polish soldiers turned toward us and peered inside, then spat on the windshield, hissing, "Jews. Thank God for war. No more Jews." Another soldier spat, then smacked the van so hard that it shook. Jews? "What are Jews?" I began to cry. My father pushed his way to the door of the van and climbed out, slamming it behind him. I watched him pace back and forth.

I once told a Polish friend about the border crossing, about the soldiers walking out of the country, spitting on our windshield, happy to witness Jews leaving. She said, "You've got to understand that the soldiers had no car, that they were bedraggled and came from very poor families, and then they passed a van full of people who seemed to have all the worldly possessions that they did not. That is the reason they demonstrated their rage to you and your family." Her interpretation was comprehensible until I thought about it later, when it occurred to me that most of the people attempting to cross the border were not Jews, that there were many more rich Poles than rich Jews. So why did the soldiers accuse us of being Jews rather than capitalists or rich fucks, thus expressing a class hatred? Did the soldiers look inside our crammed van and catch us drinking Christian babies' blood? Did we look Jewish, counting our money, our noses big and ugly? We must have looked prosperous, fur coats our currency, stashed in the back. Anita thinks that their name, Apfelbaum, may have been written on the side of the van.

But the border drama that would plague me the rest of my life was about to begin. I have reconstructed the events over and over in my mind. I see it clearly, in full color and surround-sound, as in a movie, though I'm not sure if it's my movie or Rene Clement's, or Stendahl's Napoleonic retreat from Moscow in *The Charterhouse of Parma*. Suddenly my pacing father was nowhere to be seen. My uncle Max, turning purple with rage, shouted that my father crossed the border on the running board of a Mercedes a few cars ahead of ours. I closed my eyes. Voices argued, yelled, and whispered. Soldiers shouted. We were moving now and, in a blurred instant or hour, Max announced that we were in Lithuania. I was fully awake when suddenly the Citroen stopped. My father was standing on the side of the road. I pushed the van door open and ran into his arms. He was white as a ghost. His arms couldn't hold me. I took his hand and led him back to the car. I will never forget his ashen face, the color of shame. All my life, I have searched for reasons other than the ones I know to be true. Could he really have betrayed his family, his only son? He might have entered the wooden guard house and, trying to assure all of our passage, offered them his gold wedding ring to let us through, plus a wristwatch, plus a bundle of *zloty* or dollars he had in his pocket. Then the guards could have grabbed all of it, pushed him out onto the running board of the Mercedes. They might have grabbed him, tried to hurt him, and he escaped, jumped onto that running board. He may not have had the proper documents and they pushed their rifle stocks into his belly. I was desperate for another story. Perhaps, in spite of my interpretation of his ghostlike face, hard etched in my brain, his face expressed not shame but an intolerable nausea for being forced to cross without us. But I would never know who he really was, what he might have said about the life-changing incident, or who he might have become if there had been no need to cross any border. If he did bolt at the border, leaving us to our chances, what could have driven him to his decision? A thought-free survival instinct? Did he not weigh the possibility of being discovered by us, a few cars behind? Did he plan it beforehand? It must have been a split-second decision. Had he acted based upon split-second decisions before this one? Was he hoping that our car would not get through? Did the people in the Mercedes agree to his hitching a ride with them? Why did the Mercedes people throw him out of their car and leave him by the side of the road where he stood in shame and self-hatred? Or did he ask to be dropped off? Now that he is long gone and I am once again in the neighborhood of his life story, the memories of this dark defining moment have returned to haunt me.

I don't know the extent of my family's anxiety at any of the borders we had to cross to escape, but it must have been huge and debilitating, for each crossing was a matter of life and death. I don't even know what documents or bribes were necessary or how my mother, father, and uncle handled themselves with border functionaries who could not have had too much love for a bunch of "rich Jews." Somehow, they must have obtained and carried the necessary passports, visas, proofs of birth and residency, as well as the furs, jewelry, and cash to grease every outstretched hand. They must have been aware that a life and death balance existed between offering too little or too much. A fur coat? Polish *zloty*? A diamond ring?

After Max and my mother got us out of Poland, we spent four quiet months in Sweden, waiting for some country to offer us visas. "Only New York," my mother insisted in spite of offers from several South American countries that wanted the lucrative Apfelbaum fur business and reputation. Finally an American consul general recognized the name in a pile of applications and wondered for a moment why the name Apfelbaum was familiar to him, then remembered that his wife had recently bought a mink coat from them in Warsaw. The good official put the Potok-Apfelbaum visa application on top of the list and called them in their Stockholm apartment with the good news, another in a series of improbable moments, the kind that save lives.

In our rented Stockholm apartment, we were Max and his ex-wife, Zosia, their only child, six-year-old Anita; a governess, Pani Potocka; my parents and I. Pani Potocka chose to stay in Europe, but the interpretation of Zosia's story and fate depended on who spoke of it in future years. Max and my mother insisted that Zosia, Anita's mother, chose to stay in Sweden because she, a beautiful woman, had fallen in love with a Polish diplomat. Zosia, who eventually emigrated to New York in the 1950s, claimed that Max refused to take her to America. My father said that Zosia was a whore and could not control herself after another in a series of sexual encounters from which she could not tear herself away.

Anita adds a series of events to our story. Even though our war memories differ to some degree and Zosia was never known for truth telling, Anita's Zosia story makes sense. In Stockholm, Aunt Zosia gave me a ball bearing, the letters SKF written on its little black leather case. I played with it constantly and to this day believe that its magical action was instrumental in preserving my sanity in the crossing from one world to another. SKF, Svenska Kullagerfabriken, was already a large successful manufacturer of ball bearings, one of whose corporate heads Zosia had met on a train in Poland a short time before the war started. Zosia was a beautiful woman, always on the make according to family tales, so it's easy to picture her seducing an unknown Swedish businessman traveling on the same train. From the time I was a little boy until late in her life, I found her round curvy body and her whiney Zsa Zsa Gabor voice very sexy. Whatever the connection between Zosia and the SKF man, on our arrival in Latvia, Anita tells me, Zosia called her new friend in Stockholm, related our story of escape, and asked for advice. Then, mirabile dictu, Herr SKF sent an airplane to the airport in Riga to pick us up and carry us to Sweden. Before hearing this version, I took it for granted that we drove to the airport, left the Citroen in some parking lot and paid, probably with a mink coat or two, for seats on the Riga-Stockholm flight. I still treasure the little ball bearing, which lives inside my desk drawer. From time to time, I roll the circular steel casing that holds the little ball bearings inside it, amazed that the thing spins and rolls as easily as it did when I was eight years old.

Following a border incident in March 1938, Poland presented an ultimatum to Lithuania demanding the re-establishment of diplomatic relations between the two countries; and thus the border, the one we were allowed to cross, had only recently been re-opened. Who knew? Had this not been the case, where would we have ended up? And what if Zosia had not met a man on a train months before? I had never given any thought to the appearance and availability of an airplane, which seemed to be waiting for us at an airport in Riga. Like everything else that happened after the first bombs fell, it simply happened. If it had not, we would have ended our days in a Riga ghetto, or been transported back to a death camp nearer to home. Our way out—as was the case with everyone who managed it—was fraught with the most unlikely coincidences, called miracles by

87

some, called life's improbable events by me. The fragility of a choice or decision—a few days or hours before, a few days after, choosing to enter one door rather than another, making a flight or catching the one that doesn't crash—the decision or accident, either our own or someone else's, determines entire lives. A friend whose family had also gotten out said, "They had twenty unbelievable breaks. Had there been only nineteen, they would have died."

3.

I held my father's hand as we stepped off the ferry from Ellis Island. Our feet touched America at the same moment. My mother, Max, and Anita were behind us. An airplane flew above us and I hid my face in my father's overcoat. Two people whom Max had met at the World's Fair a year before met us and brought us in two taxis to their apartment on the Upper West Side. Again an airplane buzzed overhead and I flew under a dining room table, the woman—later to become the PR lady for Maximilian Furs—laughed, pulled me out, and held me against her. I only wanted to be away from the shaking earth, the sky dense with danger, the Citroen van, betrayals; away from blood-soaked Europe, away from that language, my language, away from my parents.

Now there is a new America, no longer the America of "Give me your tired, your poor, / Your huddled masses yearning to breathe free, / The wretched refuse of your teeming shore . . ." Now much of the country seems hell bent on keeping people out or sending them back to the agonizing fate awaiting them at home. It's naïve to think that America's reluctance to share wealth, or what it defines as freedom, is a rarity. Rather, it's the nature of the beast, any beast, certainly not only the American one. But owning an American passport and a long American past, I feel as guilty as the bystanders in Germany and Poland way back then, sitting comfortably at the top of quiet peace-loving Richardson Street in Vermont, angry and embarrassed but impotent.

I imagine that there was as little to be done then as there is now. There are a few brave, moral people who risk life and livelihood to tell the truth of American dominance over any group standing in its way, comparable to the few who tried to save fellow human beings in spite of the threat of death. America was a haven then, but mostly to the likes of my well-to-do merchant family; it denied access to the equally embattled throngs on their way to annihilation.

I must consider how lucky and therefore grateful I should be that I was granted entrance in February 1940, a time when Roosevelt turned away the SS *St. Louis*, a ship of Jewish refugees, and sent it back to sure death in Jew-hating Europe. In mid-summer 1939, two-thirds of respondents to an American Gallup poll said they did not want thousands of Jewish children allowed into the US no matter how threatened their lives were in the Germany of that time. Most Western countries regarded the plight of Jewish refugees with skepticism or unveiled bigotry; for just as the oppressed easily transform themselves into oppressors once their oppression is alleviated, so do the comfortable become hardened to the plight of the victims of war, greed, and violence, still so heartbreakingly evident in most of Europe, as Syrian, African, Afghani, and Iraqi refugees endure the horror of present wars or die either in flight or in the struggle for acceptance and safety. Can evil infiltrate humanity as easily as that or can we learn to care for "the other," whoever that other is? German policy of the 1930s stated simply that it is the duty of the strong to rid the world of the weak.

What an immense number of selves make up a lifetime, and how hard it is to accept all of them. I have tried for years to reconfigure, to recreate, the father that was and the

ANDREW POTOK

son that might have been. As tempting as it is to come up with different scenarios—no war, no displacement, no borders to cross, no frantic search for another kind of life—the course of life lived is unchanging; only the handling of memories, unstable and insufficient as they are, is open to imagination. With no betrayal at the border, would my father have found other occasions to express an inner need to betray, or was it (as I have always tried to believe) a split-second blackout, a biological leap for survival, brain neurons rather than the mind responding to airplanes, bombs, and bullets? Would my father and mother have stayed together if they had remained in their familiar culture? Would he have killed her or she him? But of all the moments in my life I want most to relive and change, it is the one at my father's deathbed. I wish I could have permitted my head to rest on his chest, my hands to touch his cheeks, my eyes to fill with tears. Whatever pain he had caused me, I could have recognized the immensity of his own pain and despair.

In New York, my self-hating father gloated when, during the Eisenhower administration, a man named Goldfine was caught bribing Sherman Adams, an assistant to the president, with the gift of a vicuña coat. My father loved the fact that a Jew was acting in the precise way that anti-Semites had stereotyped Jews. My father had become strictly majoritarian, no matter how dumb the position, driving me then and now to mistrust majorities, especially self-defined moral majorities.

And then, how many people in America pay tribute to the public-intellectual Jews I admire, the Noam Chomskys, the Howard Zinns, the real heroes who are vilified for their clear-headed humanity, their progressive view of the world, their morality and activism? In our corporate media, we hear mainly from a little right of center to very right of center. Even after all my years on earth, I remain astounded by the extent of ignorance——astounded by people who are enamored of violence, hatred of the other, and wealth at any price; people who vote against their own interest. How to live an informed life when mired in the communications fog, amid the lies of government, public relations, advertising and corporate media, all lawful, even embraced by capitalism? How to live in a country that finances death by drone, or "shock and awe," that allows the police to murder people of color? How to live with millionaires and billionaires buying elections, with there being no difference between politicians and lobbyists?

Deracinated, my father's life passed as in a nightmare, in an atmosphere of gloom, frozen by memories, without joy. One of the most guilt-ridden moments in my life was when I held my father's hand twenty-five years after our arrival in the US, as he, skeletal and racked with cancer, lay in his bed, speechless and in great pain. He was hardly recognizable, his sallow skin stretched as tight as it could be without tearing apart, his eyes bulging, his hand not a human hand but a vulture's claw. He moaned softly. All his life, my father moaned. He moaned as he sat at his radio listening to the news, moaned as a greeting, a warning to anyone entering the apartment. Neurasthenia, said the doctor, but it was abysmal depression and self-hatred. His mental illness was not helped by the disdain and hatred of his wife and brother-in-law, neither of whom he could escape. Uncle Max's subterfuge, bluster, and bombast allowed him, always with a push from my mother, to assume the position of the warrior king of furs. I both looked up to Max and hated him for the damage he inflicted on my father, and yet who else was there as a model of manhood, especially since my mother constantly reminded me that my father was spineless, impotent, a nothing. Above all, she would say, your father is contagious. I still struggle not to be like him. I do fear the contagion, but internalizing one's parents is a biological given on the cellular level in spite of the most fervent wishes not to allow it.

Depression seems to have run deep in the Potok family. My London cousin Anita and I have joked about it many times in the past, noting our own tendencies in that direction, always attributing it to our Potok genes. Her mother, Pola, my father's first cousin, had separated from her husband, a Saper by name, before the war, but the three of them left Sosnowiec together in 1950 to begin their English lives. Pola had always been severely depressed, and in the 1950s she was offered a frontal lobotomy. "Father and I visited her a few hours after the operation," Anita tells me. "She was bandaged up, sitting and reading a newspaper. I think she was about sixty-five at the time. For about six months she was happy, delightful, and the sort of mother I always wanted, but she gradually reverted to being a depressed unhappy person, back to being a Potok."

My uncle Stash, my father's brother, was a very depressed man. I only vaguely remember Stash in my Warsaw childhood but spent a lot of time with him during several of my visits to London where he told me the story of the one true love of his life. Before the war, he was in love with Marysia. When the Russians deported him, he knew he would never see Marysia again. After his liberation from the Soviet labor camp and during his year-long trek through Russia and vast expanses of the Near East, he could not stop dreaming about Marysia. Two years after settling in London, he was on his way down the long escalator to the Victoria Underground Station. On the other escalator, going up, he thought he saw Marysia. "I cannot believe what I see," he told me, "but I yell her name." He takes a deep breath. "And it is she. We both think the other is dead, but we are not dead. She is there and I am there. We are never so happy. We marry immediately." Stash stops and takes out his handkerchief. "It is two years later, two years," he says, still unable to believe it, "Marysia has breast cancer and she dies."

Sitting at my father's bedside as he lay dying, I wanted to be anywhere but there. My narcissistic mind had no room for grief, especially grief for this father-betrayer. "What about me?" I thought as I sat on the edge of his bed, "I am beginning to go blind. Not only that," I thought, "but I'm not like you. I can be happy." In Vermont for just a couple of years, I had everything I wanted. I lived in a house I loved with my two children, surrounded by new friends. As I sat at my father's deathbed, I couldn't wait to get out of there, and my guilt will never leave me.

From my visual past, I remember seeing only one photograph of my father. He is in a white tuxedo jacket and tie, sitting at a dining table during a transatlantic crossing on his way to Bad Nauheim, where he went a couple of times during his last years. Though I did not like his going to Germany for a holiday, I hoped he had a mistress there or somewhere. I would now love to stare deeply into his eyes, to discover something there, perhaps pleasure that, in my filial anger, I would not have known existed. Sitting there in the photograph, he is alien to me. I never knew a father who wore a tuxedo, who sat in front of splendid dishes, who looked proud doing so. I suppose he contributed to conversations at the table. The captain's table? Did anyone nod in agreement or consider him charming? Did he seek them out on deck? What did he think of when he looked into the ocean? Surely he carried a photo of me in his wallet that he showed proudly to the others. He told me that he heard both Lenin and Trotsky speak in Switzerland, the thought of which I value. His first vote in America was for the Socialist Norman Thomas. After that, it must have been depression that pushed him from social democracy to McCarthyism, a sinkhole for self-hating miserable Jews, making me wonder if he felt like a Jew. In the many generations of

Potoks, there must have been observant ones. In Yad Vashem's long list of Potoks murdered during the Holocaust, there are many Jentas, Avrahams, Fajgas, Yaakovs, Goldas, Zalmans, and Khaims. The language spoken at my parents' home was Polish. I am amazed to learn that eighty-eight percent of Polish Jews considered Yiddish or Hebrew as their native, primary language.

Once, in New York, I followed him on the streets, hoping he had a mistress, a friend, anything, but he ended up in a small walk-in Merrill Lynch office where he, with other aging men, all of them except my father dressed in good suits and polished shoes, watched the ticker tape from the New York Stock Exchange. He must have had a different life in Poland than in America. He might have had fantasies that haunted or amused or aroused him, a piece of music or a book that made him smile or cry or interested him enough to pursue them to places he had never been. It's hard to imagine my father enjoying anything, though in New York, he walked over to St. Nick's Arena to watch men perform the sick choreography of staged wrestling. His blood must have boiled with excitement; he must have shouted, hoping for gore in that hot sweaty place as men threw one another to the ground, pulled hair, pummeled mercilessly with their fists. It might have relieved some of his frustration, depression, his hatred for his brother-in-law Max, perhaps for his wife as well. My father's mental state, depression called neurasthenia by his European doctors—might have become chemically treatable had he lived longer. On the other hand, the effects of war and displacement contributed immensely to the mental pain he suffered. How I wish he had talked, reminisced, or shared his terrible pain.

Though a lot of my life has been devoted to not being, or resembling, my father, there were times when I felt like him, was him. As I inched toward blindness, the slowness that it imposed felt like his shuffle as he walked from room to room in his old, worn slippers. My awkwardness, the little physical calamities, the dependence, the not knowing what to do, where to turn, how to express needs without losing integrity, how not to be a burden, these were our shared concerns. When I left my house and marriage, when my community of friends disappeared, I came ever closer to feeling like he must have felt as he sat and moaned by his radio, smelling of old age. Surely his isolation was worse than mine. How could I not have knelt in front of him to offer companionship and solace? If I coughed or sneezed when I was a child, it was my father who took charge. I can still feel his wet lips on my forehead, checking for fever, then the sound of the glass cups inside the doctor's black bag clinking as he walked toward Number Four Moniuszki Street to lay a dozen of the little cups on my back. In his way, my father cared.

4.

My father was born in a town named Bedzin, less than forty miles west of Krakow. The Potoks had lived there for generations, owned factories and homes. Living a fairly prosperous life, and with pre-war bourgeois expectations and no history of mobility, they undoubtedly expected to remain there for generations to come.

Bedzin was founded in the ninth century on a tributary of the Vistula in the Silesian highlands. For much of the nineteenth century, there were more Jews than Catholics in both town and county. Before September 1939, more than twenty-four thousand Jews lived precariously with thirty thousand others in this thriving industrial community. Of course, Jew hatred was as virulent in Bedzin as everywhere else in Poland. Still, every summer of my childhood, I was sent there to visit my grandparents and uncles and never heard the Polish word for Jew. Even if I heard it, I wouldn't have known what it meant, or that I was one, while most Jewish kids my age were already deep into religious studies. In a recent book, *A Small Town Near Auschwitz*, the Jews from the area who survived tell of childhoods scarred by curses and beatings by Polish children taught by priests, parents, and teachers that "the Christ-killers deserve to be hated, tormented, and wiped from the earth."

In September 1939, the German Army, followed by the SS death squads, the Einsatzgruppen, burned the Bedzin synagogue and murdered whoever among the Jews appeared in their field of vision. They created the Bedzin Ghetto in 1942 and, by the summer of 1943, most of the Jews in Bedzin were deported to the nearby German concentration camp at Auschwitz. Since Bedzin was one of the last Polish communities to be liquidated, there were a relatively large number of survivors, my grandparents not among them.

Now, Artur hires a car to take us to Bedzin, about an hour's drive from Krakow. It is not quite as polluted and dismal as it was when the Lenin steel plant was active and spewing particulates for a hundred-mile radius, but it's still grim and dirty from the remaining heavy industry in the region. The few pedestrians in the Bedzin streets still wheeze and cough as they cover their mouths and noses with handkerchiefs. It's hard to picture this ugly town in its pre-war industrial splendor. Our driver takes us to the half-destroyed, long-abandoned Potok factory, whose oil presses produced a vegetable oil marketed as Potokola and the margarine named Potokana. I had been here during my 1979 visit but now again I try to stifle tears, always ready to flow, even for the present unseen reminders of what symbolized normal times.

An old drunk leans on the loading dock of the factory, where nuts, seeds, fruits, and fiber used to be unloaded for processing. I ask him if he knows anything about this factory or the Potok family who owned it. It takes him a few moments to gather his wits.

"Knew them?" he finally slurs, "My father worked for them." He stretches his arms to touch my shoulders. "Good little Jews they were," he hiccups, proud of his tolerance, surely unaware of the term's pejorative, infantilizing connotations. "Very good to us they were," he reminisces, "decent, generous people."

A few blocks away stands the large old house, a mansion, where my grandparents lived, now converted into municipal offices, work stations, the undecorated, lifeless cubicles separated by shoulder-high partitions, nearly hiding the gorgeous parquet floors that bombard me with memories of my happy summer visits.

My uncle Stash remembered an incident from one of my summer vacations in Bedzin. "When you were five, maybe six," Stash told me years ago in his Chalk Farm London flat. "Who was there aside from your father? I think Henio and his Basia, Marek and Freda, maybe Marylka and Idek. You played with your lead soldiers under the dining room table while we drank our schnapps, and somebody said, 'Pass the pickles,' and suddenly you piped up from under the table: 'Did someone say pickles?' We laughed so hard we nearly wet our pants and your governess—who was it? Inka I think—grabbed you from under us and passed you around from hand to hand, as we tossed and hugged you, and you shrieked with pleasure."

And now I wonder why no reparations money ever came from the properties in Bedzin. Though not willingly, the Germans did pay reparations money to my mother and uncle in the 1950s, but the Poles who took over the Bedzin houses and factory that belonged to my family refused to pay, even though the expropriations were undeniable. Potoks had inhabited the place for generations, with ancestral houses and a factory that produced oils exported even to America. In fact, Poland never repaid anyone anything, at first claiming poverty, then, after joining the European Union and becoming the wealthiest among Eastern European nations, considering itself the apogee of victimhood, Poland simply refused to acknowledge that it took possession of property, especially that of murdered or displaced Jews.

Back in Krakow, I ask Artur why we're suing a relative of mine to get possession of an ugly little apartment house rather than suing the Polish government for taking over the factory and making offices from a beautiful old mansion where my family lived. "I advise you to forget about the Bedzin property. You could hire a Polish lawyer," he says, "who would charge you a lot of money and then," he says, "I promise you that nothing will come of it."

"Nothing will come of it? Why?"

"I think because they do not have to." He says nothing for a moment, then, "Because once that starts, there will be no end to it. Believe me, Andrew, there is nothing to be done."

Andy, age two,
with his father,
Leon Potok, 1933

A happier time, before
the war: the author, age
six, in the Potoks'
apartment on Moni-
uszki Street in Warsaw,
1937

In Warsaw's beautiful Lazienki Park, Anita and Andy, ages six and four, with Anita's mother, Zosia, 1937

Dressed to kill, young Andy walking to the park on Marszalkowska, 1938

Safe at last in Stockholm, a month before boarding the Norwegian ship *Bergensfjord,* bound for New York, 1940

The author's father, Leon Potok, with Anita, age fourteen, and Andy, age sixteen, in the Potoks' New York apartment, 1947

Uncle Max, Anita's father, standing in front of his Lincoln Continental, New York City, 1948

Anna Potok, Andy's mother,
surrounded by her beautifully
designed fur coats in a back
room of Maximilian Furs, 1960

From the collection of Marjorie
Witherspoon: *Molivos*, a Potok
abstract oil on canvas, in reds,
yellows, greens, and blues, 62 in. x 48
in., 1965

Created near the end of his visual art career, *Portal*, a large wood mockup (before being manufactured in steel), painted black and red, displayed on the grounds of a Waitsfield, Vermont, museum, 1970

Potok in his Vermont studio, 1970

Partially sighted, Potok writing his book *Ordinary Daylight* with the help of a closed-circuit TV system, 1978

Loie on the Mendocino Headlands, her favorite place on earth, 1984

With his mother, Anna, then in her early eighties, on the back lawn of Andy's house, 1980

The Necklace, oil on canvas, 40 in. x 30 in., a double portrait of Andy and Loie, which Andy painted with just a shred of eyesight left, two years after Loie's return to his life, 1998

Potok with his son, Mark, and grandson, Nickie, in their Montgomery, Alabama, house, 2000

Seventy-one years later, revisiting Ellis Island, 2001

Potok with his daughter, Sarah, grandchildren Anna and Rachel, Sarah's guide dog Flan, and the author's guide dog Tobias, Santa Barbara, 2004

Potok with Tobias, sneaking a touch of a bas-relief at the National Gallery of Art, Washington, DC, 2004

Andy and Loie sailing
down the Hudson River
in her father's boat,
Sonni, 2006

The author with his children, Mark and Sarah, Montgomery,
Alabama, 2010

In the living room of their
Montpelier, Vermont, house,
Andy and Gabriel, 2013

13 Stradomska Street, Krakow, Poland, 2014

The author in
2016

7

THE AMBIGUITY OF BETRAYALS

1.

Back in the Hotel Rubinstein, as Loie sleeps and a hint of klezmer music wafts in from a few blocks down Szeroka Street through the badly fitted Hotel Rubinstein windows, I have a conversation with my grandmother Paulina and grandfather Solomon on whose streets I have been walking for days. They are sitting on the two chairs in front of the hotel windows. In his deep gravelly voice, my grandfather tells me that Bedzin was so close to the German border that the Wehrmacht was on the Bedzin streets the first or second day of the invasion. "It was a cloudy, dark day," Solek, my *dziadek* says. "I knew that those Germans were beasts but I needed a cigarette. Can you imagine anyone so addicted to tobacco? I thought I could make it to Kaminska's store, not very far from our house. My voice was beginning to sound like that of an old man. I coughed and wheezed. You would think I was smarter than that." I think of my own addictions. I could not have resisted, just as he could not, perhaps not a cigarette but a late afternoon martini or a woman awaiting me. "The German was not very young," my grandfather continues, "perhaps a decent man, maybe a teacher or salesman or mechanic, but with a cruel thin mouth and hollow eyes. He stuck out his chest and yelled 'Juden!' Is he talking to me? I thought. Then he shot me and I was gone after the third bullet."

My grandmother's hair is swept back into a neat gray bun. Her face is lined with age, her soft arms cool as they were in the heat of a Bedzin summer. "My poor Solek never knew how lucky he was to get it over so quickly," she now tells me. "After he was gone, they dragged me to the woods where Jewish old men with their prayer shawls and side-locks as well as two Jewish children hung from trees. The soldiers pointed and laughed. I screamed and they poked their guns into my stomach, and dragged me into a ghetto. I am hardly Jewish. You know, my Jendrush, we were never practicing Jews. We were—how do you say it?—agnostics. And then, from the ghetto to Auschwitz. I will say no more."

"Before all that, did you shop in their shops? How did you manage to live and work among the people who hated you?"

"No, no," my grandmother objects, wagging her finger at me. "Not all of them hated us. We had friends among them."

I turn to one side and try to sleep, knowing that there are no Jews left in Bedzin, very few in Krakow. I cannot comprehend those who survived the camps or exile else-where, then chose to return, reminders of the largely for-gotten past, the once despised minority, a challenge to the concept of Polishness, a puzzling presence, Zulus or Eski-mos, clowns with their yarmulkes and sidelocks.

Shortly before this trip, I read *Fear*, a book by Jan Gross, in which he writes that approximately 250,000 Polish Jews returned home immediately after the war, mostly from the Soviet Union, and were subjected to a wave of violence and hostility; up to 1,500 were murdered in either individual actions or in pogroms. With most of the three million Polish Jews already slaughtered, a pogrom flared up in Kielce, after that town had been completely "cleansed of Jews." Two hundred former Jewish residents who had survived the concentration camps returned, forty of them, accused of "blood libel," were clubbed to death by a mob of workers from a nearby steel mill and gunned down by police and soldiers. The mob then stormed the hospital, where they murdered injured Jews and, during the next few months, killed thirty more, while Catholic priests, bishops, and cardinals condoned the killing, blaming the Jews for their involvement in the Communist hierarchy, as well as citing their belief that the "blood libel" accusation was never proven false. Even Pope Pius XII, still going strong in spite of his friendship with the Nazis, refused to admonish the Polish church.

When friends remind me that I should not make black and white proclamations about Polish guilt, I cannot get the images of Kielce out of my mind. Surely not all Poles were capable of this level of brutality. Surely Jews returning to other towns or villages were not slaughtered. And then I wonder, does this degree of violence happen elsewhere, not just in Poland? Of course it does. For starters, take the Greenwood section, all black, of Tulsa, Oklahoma in 1921— a mere twenty years before some of the Polish brutality— where up to three hundred people were slaughtered and eight hundred injured, all by white fellow residents of Tulsa. Human hatred knows no bounds. Many Poles seem to resent that Polish behavior during and after the war gets reduced in the minds of many Westerners to a narrative about the fate of the country's Jews. That was not the only story, they say, nor was the Jewish story generally confined to Poland. All of that is true. Poles have had more than their share of suffering, and many Poles risked their lives by protecting and saving Jews. There are many sides to every story, but as a Jew affected by the history of World War II, I can only write what is apparent to me and what has always been apparent to Jewish populations in this part of the world. Certainly a lot more anger and blame are due the Germans and Austrians, the perpetrators of unimaginable hate and violence, but that fact does not translate into letting Polish anti-Semitism off the hook. Poland was not responsible for the war or for a policy of annihilation of Jews. Conditions and choices were absolutely horrendous for all sorts of peoples in the wretched eastern European lands, and perhaps the main motivation in looking at Kielce and Jebwabne and other murder sites in Poland should be to probe the depths of the human, rather than just the Polish, capacity for bad faith and outright evil. To be sure, the events in Poland had a specific history, which needs to be accounted for, but not in the mode of those people being distinctly evil, and the rest of us smugly not. As regards American behavior in the world, the number of war criminals at the very top of the US government disallows judgment of the behavior of any other nation. When we accuse other nations of blatant criminal acts, spouting platitudes about American exceptionalism, the hypocrisy is blatant, laughable. Nations tend to perform criminal acts, with very few exceptions. Even though one can point to the decency of the Danes in protecting Danish Jews in the war, heroic acts in face of the probable punishment from the Germans, even little Denmark cannot be counted on to continue moral behavior throughout its history. Danish attitudes toward Syrian refugees tilts even them toward the other side of the morality scale.

The great Polish poet Zbygniew Herbert, in the wake of the Second World War, warned his fellow countrymen of the need for precision about the millions murdered.

. . . it was a long time ago
a wind mixed up the ashes . . .
but in these matters
accuracy is necessary
one can't get it wrong
even in a single case . . .
ignorance about those who are lost
undermines the reality of the world . . .

2.

Learning from Artur that the Potok born in 1830 had sixteen children by two wives is worth a smile, nothing more, but knowing that not only my father but a nephew of my grandmother's, Edward Prokocimer, was capable of betrayal is not easy to live with. As I have learned so painfully during my more than eighty years of life, practically no one escapes betrayal, small or large.

Is it just that there is a rotten egg in everyone's family? I have tried to vindicate my father's act by questioning my memory and then, in my last book, I fictionalized him into the father I might have had, a father whose betrayal I made ambiguous and pardonable, a father I could love.

Uncle Max, not exactly an innocent in the betrayal camp, was a rager and a brawler, a man among men; a card playing, handsome, womanizing man, as well as a hand-kissing valet to the rich, at times backstabbing and mean. Maximilian Apfelbaum, who became Michael Maximilian in New York—"for business reasons," my mother said—had a checkered history. Years later, my mother told me that Max had not even wanted to save Zosia from the Germans by taking her with us in the Citroen van in Warsaw. "Not until I told him that Zosia is the mother of Anita, his own daughter, and we must pick her up and save her." I will never know who was telling the truth, since the troika of uncle Max, mother Anna, and father Leon preferred secrets and lies to openness and clarity.

Though no betrayal can compare with the big one that haunts this part of the world, the European betrayal of Jews, memories of past betrayals flood my mind after another day in Krakow. Is it the need for a final reckoning at this late time in my life or the hostile March winds or my awareness of Loie's discomfort about being in Poland? I wonder how much my family's betrayals, their secrets and lies, their need to dismiss the past have influenced my bad decisions, my leaps into and out of marriages, careers, moods, whatever seemed right or captivating at the moment. I wonder how the parenting I received has affected my feelings about human capacities, the depth of my loves and hates, my commitment to art, friendship, marriage, and my own parenting abilities.

I was still in architecture school when, in 1954, Joan and I married. Her parents, my in-laws, never came to terms with their Oklahoma daughter marrying a Jewish refugee artist. After a year, Joan and I moved to Paris where I found a job drafting the most boring of interior spaces for the first ugly high-rises to be built on the outskirts of the city. My beautiful wife and I played house, both of us too young and stupid to do otherwise. Shortly after we settled in a dingy apartment near the Trocadero, we discovered Joan was pregnant. Although my given reason for not wanting children was the madness of nuclear proliferation and the armaments race, it's clear to me now that, having had the kind of parenting I wish I could forget, I did not want to indulge in the questionable activity of child rearing. My mother came to Paris for the fall collections, and when Joan told her that she was pregnant, my mother's immediate response was, "My dear, I know a very good abortionist." That did it. Joan carried our son Mark to term.

We moved to Italy for the summer. While Joan was unknowingly pregnant again, she rode on the back of my motorcycle while Anita drove baby Mark in her English Ford to Barcelona from which we all sailed to the island of Mallorca. Soon after we rented a house in a suburb of Palma, we heard that people were fleeing the Communist regime in Hungary. Anita was the first to go. "I need to be there," she said. "It's up to us refugees to help." A week later, I took a boat to Barcelona, then traveled twenty kilometers south of Vienna by train to the Traiskirchen refugee camp, which was already crowded beyond its capacity. Anita ran a kindergarten and I helped distribute clothing. We were both shocked when, some days later, Joan arrived. She had left our one-year-old son with nuns. "With nuns?" I asked, incredulous.

"They'll take good care of him," she said, but when we returned to Mallorca a few weeks later, the nuns, thinking we would never come back, had given Mark to a local family. When we finally found and claimed him, the expression on his face was surely a replica of mine when I saw my father standing at the side of the road in Lithuania. My little one-year-old baby was betrayed, and I will never forgive myself for being even an unknowing part of it. For the first time, I thought about the anguish that must have entered my father's heart for the remaining twenty-seven years he lived after the Lithuanian border incident.

When Mark was six and our daughter Sarah was four, Joan and I moved to the island of Mytilini in the northeast Aegean and, a year later, rented a house in a suburb of Athens. Toward the end of our second year in Greece, as I was about to fly back to New York with a bunch of rolled up paintings to be stretched on wooden frames and exhibited, Joan asked me if I intended to come back. I said I didn't know, and she didn't seem particularly upset. We were getting bored with each other, outgrowing our nine-year marriage, and soon after my arrival in New York, Joan wrote that she was falling in love with an American marine archeologist. She moved in with Peter, and it didn't take long for her to become pregnant. She was much happier, as it turned out, with a warrior-sailor-archeologist than a still-unrecognized painter. She soon extolled "men and machines," and became Peter's lieutenant, learning to map the remains of sunken ships at the bottom of the Aegean and, later, the Adriatic. "That's the way the cookie crumbles," said Captain Peter to a friend, describing the breakup of my marriage and the establishment of his. By mutual agreement, Mark and Sarah, now eight and six, flew back to America with me.

In New York, I bought an old Renault and we drove up to Vermont to visit Anita, who had settled there a few years before. As Mark, Sarah, and I pulled up to a Texaco station in the village of Plainfield, Charlotte, who became my second wife a few years hence, happened to walk by on her way to a meeting at the local college where she worked. My crappy little Renault, bought a week before from a car lot in Queens, had just barely made it all the way north and, cooling down, began spitting parts of itself onto the pavement. Charlotte approached, smiled, and, as she passed by, ran one finger from my wrist to my elbow with just the right amount of pressure, the hottest of promises that, over very little time, blossomed into a rich relationship.

Not long after I arrived in Vermont, Joan wrote asking for a quick divorce. She wanted the first child of her second litter to be legal in the eyes of her church. "The Greeks will agree to it if you have the divorce papers well decorated with wax seals and ribbons," she wrote. After the legal documents were exquisitely beribboned, waxed, and stamped, we agreed that the kids would continue to live with me and spend every summer with Joan and Peter, sailing and diving for treasure on the bottom of the sea.

I fell in love with a run-down farmhouse and the hundred acres that came with it. The old house's clapboards were rotting, its roofline was concave, the bricks of its former chimney were mostly gone. Inside, the windowpanes were hand blown, bull's-eye marks refracting the sunlight that poured in. Spidery gas fixtures hung on many walls, which were insulated with corncobs. There wasn't a right angle in the place, not the unpainted clapboards, not the old roof, not a window or a door, and yet it was a refugee's dream, with a multitude of trees, meadows—American soil. I loved the entire package for its decrepitude and its distance from my father's depression, from Maximilian Furs, from the whole fucking Upper East Side; a safe distance from the fancy ladies, their overbred dogs, children and husbands. From both the front and the back of the house, I could see for miles downhill. Neither fashion world limousines nor unfriendly tanks could surprise me. But it did not take long to discover that the woman who owned the General Store in the village hated Jews, though she did it nicely by suggesting that we spend Sundays at her Methodist church. People here still "Jewed you down." The local progressive college was "a nest of Jews, while the lovely hills were beginning to be transformed and polluted by downcountry Jews. Still this was not Poland. A little patience was required, a little waiting and smiling before taking one's place as artisan, farmer, artist; to doff overalls and shitkicker boots, attend their town meetings, buy lawn mowers at Montgomery Ward's, grow zucchinis, sit in trees waiting for deer.

In back of the house, past a few butternut trees and an old stone fence, the kids and I sat in the middle of a huge meadow, the village way below us, blue mountains on the distant horizon. We heard the sound of a truck downshifting in the village, then a freight train on its way north, whistling at a far-off railroad crossing. These spare, discrete counterpoints of comforting noises, together with the visual arpeggios of sunlight lighting up tin roofs one after the other, and a line of poplars introducing an architectural order into the unruly woods below, were as reassuring to a city dweller like me as a traffic light in a busy intersection.

It was a joy putting Mark and Sarah on the yellow school bus every morning and waiting for them to be dropped off every afternoon. Giving them a home, reading to them, playing games with them, but especially giving them a language, a language we could speak together, play with, explore, has always been in the forefront of my mind as the greatest of all gifts. Every June I drove them to New York and put them on a plane bound for Greece where they spent the summer with their mother and her new husband. Men and boys being favored by both Peter and Joan, Mark's summers were happy, with sailing and diving, while Sarah, a dispensable female, was left to fend for herself. When she came home at the end of each summer, gloomy and angry, I didn't understand the seriousness of her neglect and abandonment. Who knows what to call Joan's leaving one-year-old Mark with the Mallorquin nuns or her neglect of Sarah? As I did, Joan wanted our kids to grow up strong, independent, fearless.

I was hardly a stranger in the landscape of betrayal. Twenty-five years after Charlotte and I married, I fell prey to what now appears to be a family trait. How to justify it? Oh, so many excuses, almost reasons for flight, for seeking change. How about the end of an evolutionary passion for reproduction, a burgeoning creative urge, a newly felt need to take a major risk? I had begun to paint again, and I felt rejuvenated, the possessor of a new power. Risk taking had been severely reduced by the care and caution imposed by blindness, and now the joys of risk taking were again in the air. And there she was, a young woman who wanted only to furnish intellectual spice to my predictable life. She loved reading to me daily, loving the material. She announced baseball games with knowledge and humor. Her love of art was genuine as, eventually, was her interest in giving and taking erotic pleasure. After more than a year of daily reading to me in my office, my reader told me that she was in love with me. How could anyone as tuned in to female sensibilities as I was could have missed the electricity that must have permeated our daily lunch hours together? I was in my early sixties with only a shred of eyesight left, not precisely an image—at least in my mind—of a lover, especially to a woman more than thirty years younger than I.

Leaving the marriage was giving up years of learning to live in relative peace with another human being, with its shared ups and downs, the good times earned by sustaining the difficult times, the carefully constructed give and take, the allowances for infractions and even little betrayals, the opportunity to keep building on what there was and, absolutely essential to my happiness, a community of friends that was full of love, warmth, conviviality, conversation, exchange, learning, and reciprocity.

The moment of a final decision was upon me, the pull in both directions seemed equal, the strength of a feather capable of pushing me one way or the other. Although the comparison did not occur to me at the time, I now wonder if my betrayal-waiting-to-happen was in any way comparable to my father's moment at the Lithuanian border. His was a thoughtless, unfathomably selfish choice of personal survival. Was mine, though perhaps trivial in order of magnitude, as selfish as his, based on fantasies of pleasure? Movement rather than stasis? Curiosity? A magic bullet. I inflicted pain everywhere, on Charlotte, on the young woman whose promises were so tantalizing, on the community of friends whose responses to my action were devastating. "One does not leave a woman in her sixties," said an old friend, a part of my life since college, in her sixties herself. "Fuck your young woman as much as you like," she said, "but don't leave the marriage."

A close friend, a writer with whom I had shared my work as he shared his with me, was outraged and began treating me with anger and disdain. "I thought that friends remain friends even though from time to time we may disapprove of each other's behavior," I said.

"Wrong. You are a friend until you do something I find morally repugnant," he hissed at me and slammed my office door.

Aloneness turned out to be my hell, and though blindness did not help, it was only one of many reasons for feeling destitute, empty, hopeless. Blind people do live alone, often with dignity and grace. As a child, I liked being alone. The careers I have chosen are lonely ones but, at the end of the day, there was company. During the few years between Joan and Charlotte, I had cherished being alone, though with my children and friends nearby who filled my life with warmth and love.

A year living with Karen had its ecstatic pleasures, intellectual and sexual, as well as its sometimes trying adjustments to another person, with her unique history, neuroses, and obsessions, compounded by the fact that I'd had sixty-three years of life by that time, and Karen only thirty. Even though we were each acquainted with the other's songs, Karen's were harder for me, the old dog, to adjust to than, I think, mine were for her. Our mutual interest in literature, the visual arts, and sports was intoxicating, sometimes comical. "He's showing bunt," Karen would announce as she watched and I listened to a baseball game on television, or "It's in the dirt!"

My children, Mark and Sarah, both older than Karen, were outraged, as were my friends and Charlotte's children, my step-children, Jed and Maya. Charlotte was grief-stricken, enraged and humiliated, quite unprepared for the direction my actions had imposed on her. With the help of a few friends, she burned the sheets we'd slept on and kept on making exciting, often whimsical pottery. She continued to live in a smaller house built for her by her son Jed on our fabulous property and, fourteen years later, in 2008, died of heart disease and lung cancer.

In the middle of our first summer together, Karen, a Shakespeare scholar, left for New York, where she had been offered the directorship of a student production of *All's Well That Ends Well*. In her absence, I began to realize not only that I was filling her need for a father figure but that, as wonderful as Karen was, we came from very different worlds, an abyss that would deepen into misery on both our parts. Why was this happening? I chose not to live with Charlotte and now I was choosing not to live with Karen. They both loved me. Karen seemed to thrive on my blindness, my dependence. I knew I couldn't live alone and now I was proving that I couldn't live with anyone. After swallowing a few—very few—sleeping pills, I ended up in the ER room where some sort of charcoal cocktail eventually cleared my gut of poison.

I moved to a dismal apartment in Montpelier from which I walked for miles with my guide dog Topper to and from a psychoanalyst who showed little understanding or tolerance for my misery. My life hit rock bottom. As I sobbed on his corduroy couch, he demonstrated empathy by bringing me a box of man-sized Kleenex, then returned to sit silently in his chair. Toward the end of one of my miserable sessions with this silent recipient of my grief, he picked up his phone and called the hospital psych ward. Turning away from me, he arranged for my incarceration.

"Me?" I said, stirring from the couch. Topper sat up, ears perked. "You're sending me to the psych ward? The loony bin? What are they going to do to me?" I had mentioned suicide once or twice but, as usual, curiosity about the next world outrage won out. It was the mid-1990s, with Timothy McVeigh in Oklahoma City, O. J. Simpson in California, the Serbs in Srebrenica. So if not suicide, how to survive? A few days before, as my arms were numbing from the wrists to the elbows, I felt as if, finally and for all time, I was going mad. Perhaps the loony bin made sense.

"I'll call you when you're settled in," Dr. Shithead promised.

In the hospital, nurses came in and out of my room with pills served in little paper containers, and dragged me to intensely depressing group meetings featuring the psychologist-in-chief asking the one vital question: "Mr. Potok, did you take your meds today?"

Karen went on to have a successful life in the theater. As for Dr. Shithead, I should not have been surprised that he never called. My two-week incarceration simply changed the location of my misery.

And then, as close to a miracle, a deus ex machina, as it could possibly be, on the day before I was to be discharged from my two weeks in the loony bin, Loie called. I had not heard her voice for twenty-five years, and it took a few moments to fully understand who was on the other end of the phone line. She had come to Vermont to see old friends. "Everyone I met in the streets told me that you were not in good shape and that I'd be a rotten person if I didn't call you."

That night, for the first time in decades, I recalled our brief time together. How did I keep her magnificent image out of my mind for so long? Memories of Loie hovered not only in the brain stem to be called up when searching for erotic events, but in the finer frontal lobe where quieter emotions simmered. I couldn't picture her body aging. But me? Twenty-five years before, I was driving, my hair was black, my own body lean and strong, all the teeth in my mouth mine. Now, blind and nearly bald, with white hairs poking out of nose and ears, fingernails striated and gums retracted, I recalled a story about Felix Mendelssohn's grandfather, the philosopher Moses Mendelssohn, and his first meeting the woman whom he knew he wanted as his wife. She was shocked when she saw that he was a little weakling with a hunchback and a huge nose, anything but handsome. Standing there, facing each other, he told her that God had ordained that it was she who was to be born deformed, but that he had prayed to God to give him the hunchback and let her grow up straight. This not only touched her, but won her. She became his wife and bore him many children.

And so, a few days later, Loie knocked on my door. After hours of catching up, she lay down on the couch and I kneeled beside her. I couldn't stop smiling. My fingers felt her lips, smiling as well. Little by little, we touched more of each other, blotting out the dissatisfaction, grimness, and loneliness in each of our lives. And, wonder of wonders, Loie never left.

8

TESTIMONY

1.

At the Hotel Rubinstein now, I try to shove all the betrayals from center stage, but as much as I try to keep my anger at bay, being in Poland brings previously unexpressed angers back with a vengeance. As Loie and I lie in bed, I reach out to touch her and try to find a pleasant topic. I tell her how much I'm enjoying hearing spoken Polish, my first language, its complicated sound a kind of music to my ears. Unable to sleep much in Krakow, my brain had begun recapturing forgotten words, declensions, conjugations. At breakfast in the morning, I give it a try, speaking it slowly, the acrobatics of tongue and teeth formidable. This high-wire act of crowded consonants, once so fluid and painless, now emerge like strands of meat forced through a grinder. Nevertheless, everyone responds to my efforts with exaggerated praise. "You speak so well," they tell me, "so very well." And I feel proud.

Mid-morning, Loie and I walk from Kazimierz to the center of Krakow, the second largest and one of the oldest cities in Poland, dating back to the seventh century. It is a center of Polish academic, cultural, and artistic life, the capital of Poland from 1038 to 1569. The March weather continues to be lousy, cold and windy with snow on the streets and sidewalks. It's a bad time to be in Poland. Still, I want Loie to get a taste of this very old and beautiful city, its Gothic, Renaissance, and Baroque architectural magnificence, the beautiful Vistula River flowing through it, surrounded by richly wooded landscapes. In my previous visit to Krakow, I still had some vision and loved walking from its Old Town to its perimeter. Here, until the war, 68,000 Jews lived, a quarter of Krakow's population, most of them in the district of Kazimierz, which was more or less deeded to them in the thirteenth century. As soon as the Germans occupied Krakow in 1939, they built a ghetto across the Vistula River, and from there the train ride to Auschwitz was less than one hour. Today there are two hundred Jews left in Krakow.

In the medieval Market Square, Rynek Glowny, we find a bookstore where I long to get my hands on a children's book that was read to me when I was a little boy by its author, Julian Tuwim, a friend of my family and an important poet of the time. When I tell the saleslady that I sat on Tuwim's lap as he read me *Lokomotywa* (Locomotive), she is almost in tears. She tells me that the book, written in the thirties, is still a children's favorite. Some of the words of the poem "Lokomotywa" have remained with me all my life, its language aping the deep sounds of the huge iron gorilla of a train, chugging and huffing, then gathering speed, rumbling, then flowing through the Polish countryside. I suspect that the rhythm of stressed and unstressed syllables of "Lokomotywa" and other Tuwim poems influenced my love of one particular lilt and flow of speech rather than another, as much as the horse chestnuts of the Saski Gardens influenced my love of paint.

This thirteenth-century square, the largest in Europe, the greatest tourist attraction in Krakow, is almost deserted, piles of snow and ice and howling wind making every step hazardous. On our way to an open café, we are accosted by a sleazy guy who offers a free lunch at McDonald's if we take his tour of Auschwitz.

"I'm going to kick his ass," Loie says. Another guy cuts in with an offer of pizza for his Auschwitz tour. Loie lets go of me and, as I imagine her pulling her arm back to slug him, the man flees. Loie's arms and legs are very strong, thanks to her years of work at a coop bakery in Berkeley. "I hate this place," she says as we duck into a bustling restaurant for hot soup. I want Loie to see Auschwitz, only thirty miles from here, probably as foolish a desire as the wish for the beloved to be excited by one's birthplace. This is where you went to summer camp? Wow! The bushes where you made out with your girlfriend? Auschwitz is no more mine than hers, but I want to share this tribal grave with my wife even though I don't do graves, not individual ones, not those of celebrity writers or other heroes, not my father's. Not only that but I have mixed emotions about mass graves whose purpose is to concentrate the mind on the events that took place there, to soak up the miasma of horror, to have done with it, get over it, restore contentment, to have a transcendent experience, an epiphany, all of which might be better accomplished elsewhere.

My first time at Auschwitz was with Anita, who never forgave me for dragging her there. Our 1979 Auschwitz visit was, in fact, degrading. This killing ground, so well chosen by the German corporate beasts (although the existence of train tracks could have placed the death camp in many different places, and a minimum of local opposition could have been assured most anywhere in the country), was transformed into a museum. The blockhouses, the living quarters in which people had been stacked, were now cottages named for the many nationalities who contributed victims to the ovens. All European nations were represented except for Jews who, in fact, were not a nation. Off to the side, largely unseen and locked, stood a Jewish house whose entrance was unlocked only for groups considered to be large enough to disturb an Auschwitz functionary's time away from painting her fingernails. When she did appear to perform this bothersome task of turning a key, her disgust was visible, her nose scrunched as if by a stinking outhouse.

Inside this "Jewish pavilion" the exhibition of photographs and artifacts was stunningly and movingly exhibited, but the feeling of being in enemy territory remained thick as the stench of rotten fish. In the structures designated by the names of Czechoslovakia, Romania, Bulgaria, and the rest, the displays of crutches and eyeglasses and vats of human hair were moving but pristine, like the British Museum's ancient trinkets or masks from Africa. Even knowing that some of our family were put to death here did not eclipse the gentility of the raked paths, the barren but not unpleasant landscape, the picture postcards and now probably T-shirts.

Loie and I do not go to Auschwitz. That evening, rain and wind still howling outside the doors of the Hotel Rubinstein, we run across the street to the restaurant Shara, which is nearly deserted. Loie is not only tired but grumpy. "This weather is too much," she says. We are shown to a table by a woman with a few basic English words, kielbasa and vodka primary among them. I remember the Polish words for potatoes and herring. She understands soup. "Did you want to go to Auschwitz at all?" I ask my wife.

"Of course I did," she says, sounding a little annoyed, "but you're a mess. I didn't think you could make it." The waitress brings herring in sour cream, and two little shot glasses of vodka. "Take mine too," Loie says. Gladly, I polish them off. "I hate this place," Loie says again.

"The restaurant?"

"Poland," she says. "Do you realize what a mess you've been? You're furious with everyone and everything. If anyone touched you, you'd smack them." I fold up my white cane and plunk it noisily under the table. "Look, honey," she says, "I'm not blaming you. You're mourning for your lost family. I'm just saying that it's been hard for me too. The place makes me feel like a wandering Jew."

"Your roots are here too." Even though Loie's father was born in Czestochowa, he and his family escaped earlier in the century after a series of pogroms. I went to Czestochowa during my previous trip to Poland and hated the place, home to the Polish Catholic icon, their Black Madonna, and a pilgrimage site like Lourdes in France, crutches hanging on the church's walls, testaments to the power of simplemindedness.

My mouth is stuffed with kielbasa and cabbage, and I'm ravenous for the dish of boiled potatoes waiting on the side. "It's amazing that you love Polish food," Loie says, not yet touching the plate of herring in front of her. "Your mother never cooked." I'm chewing and say nothing. "Right?" she asks.

I look down at the food and I'm struck with the lack of sensual memories from this place except for the eroticism of the horse chestnuts in the Saski Gardens. Is there not a single smell or taste that brings me the ecstatic nostalgia for childhood I hear so much about? From my many weeks with one governess or another, I cannot even recapture the smell of pines in Zakopane, or of lilacs and lilies in the meadows of Otwock, or the ocean smells of Gdynia. I love the taste of borscht, kielbasa, and pierogi, but these tastes, together with chicken Kiev, were born in the Russian Tea Room, not the *pensions* of Rabka or of Number Four Moniuszki. Jewish cooking was probably banned from my parents' kitchen as were Yiddish, rabbis, and talk of ghettos or shtetls. I'm afraid that aromas and tastes disappeared together with the sense of family, probably embedded in the unreachable neurons of the amygdala. So what remains in the nostrils or the tongue? Fantasies of revenge, hatred, and anger.

During my previous time in Poland, I met the movie director P., a beloved troublemaker who, at that time of Soviet occupation, was treasured by sophisticated people, victims of oppression, scholars of allegory and allusion, and experts in partitions, insurrections, and consolidations who were eager to mock, if not yet overthrow, the moribund Soviet regime. Clearly, the arts had an urgency beyond the aesthetic. Art and poetry were dangerous, and I envied all of these artist-fighters' life and death struggle with totalitarian ideology, and the small, furtive, cultural guerilla actions that inflicted casualties. Although I couldn't possibly keep up with his intake of vodka, I had greatly enjoyed his company, our bantering about life and art; I loved the Polishness of the man, a jolly freedom fighter.

I call P. in Warsaw and the next day he drives down in his little Polish Fiat to spend a day with us. He has a favorite bar in Krakow named Spokoj (meaning peace) where, as in the bars of Warsaw, he loved being among artists and would-be artists. Down a long passage and up some stairs, he is immediately recognized, "not so much for the films I now make," says he, "but the former me." P. is known not only as a clever movie maker but a lifelong drunk, the latter characterization not terribly special among the Polish literati.

I heard that soon after Solidarity took over and Poland leaped happily back into the market economy, P., no longer the darling of the oppressed, drifted easily into television commercials in which near-naked women sprawled lusciously over Ford and Chevy hoods. Freed from one oppression, he seemed to enjoy mucking about in another.

"Do you miss the thrill of making idiots of the censors?" I ask him.

"I have learned to tolerate change," he says and downs the first hundred grams of vodka. "Speaking of change,

Andrew," he says, "when I visited you in Vermont, you were thinking of painting again. I tell everyone I know about my blind American friend who paints."

"I painted for a few years. It was pure joy but I stopped when my eyes totally gave out."

"What did they look like?" P. asks Loie, who has been silent until now, probably people watching, one of her most pleasurable activities.

"I love them," she says, "a series of canvasses; all of them figure paintings including a portrait of me which actually looks like me."

"So," he says, "no more abstraction?"

"I'm thinking that any old blind guy can lay on colors, mush them around. Not me, not this blind guy. So I found a narrative."

"Narrative? What narrative?"

"An old goat, me, a fleshy seductive woman, Loie, a young buck waiting in the background."

P. yells to someone in Polish a few tables away, raises his glass, and continues with me. "So how did you do it?" he asks.

"I Brailled the color name on the tube, squeezed globs onto a glass palette in a given order. Loie had come into my life at the time."

Loie is nursing a glass of white wine. "Benny Goodman is blaring on the CD player," she says, "Andy is wiggling his ass to the music, the happiest I've ever seen him."

"My arms and hands remembered how to paint," I tell him, "and with the smell of oils and turps in my nostrils, I felt as alive as a kid flying on his first bicycle ride."

He raises his drink and the three of us clink glasses. A group of hippie types ambles over and they high-five P., who is in his element. He introduces them to us and, in my defensive mode, I wonder which of them hates Jews— another unpleasant, suspicious moment in my Krakow psyche because, after the group of artists and wannabe artists go back to their table, P. tells us, perhaps because he has read the interior of my deranged mind, that the best filmmakers in Poland are Jewish. "Isn't that wonderful?" he asks, then adds, "Who is it that said that there is hope only in art, that in reality there is none? We have art in order not to die of the truth." He bends his head back and downs another vodka, then orders a bottle of champagne. "I made four movies, a couple of shorts, some TV shit. It's been good. I miss Poland in the bad old days but it's really better now." He pours three flutes of champagne. "I'm more serious now," he says, "more thoughtful, not a clown, but I still love having the players improvise. Remember Lolek? He really liked you. Well, he's become a first-class actor."

P. brings a wonderful part of Poland back into focus. I don't think we ever spoke about the so-called Jewish problem either in Warsaw or Vermont. I admire this man immensely and can't imagine him hating anyone.

After a couple most pleasant hours, we follow him to his car. In spite of the alcohol P. consumed, he insists on driving us back to the hotel, and from there, in spite of our begging him to stay the night, he drives the several hours back to Warsaw.

2.

Artur picks us up in his sporty Mercedes to drive us to the courthouse where he introduces us to his partner, Marcin, and a female translator, Katarzyna, whose English is perfect. She and I talk of the poet Tuwin, whose children's books she knows well. "Men and women in black robes are running from office to office," Katarzyna says. "I don't know how the women do it wearing high heels." I listen to the high heel clatter with some pleasure, a syncopated polyphony.

"Very cute," Loie says. "Under their robes, tight jeans and spike heels." We are called into chambers, and before entering Artur's partner puts on a black robe, which, so the translator tells me, lawyers are required to wear. "Jesus, Andy, Artur is not putting on a robe," Loie whispers in my ear.

"Oh shit, it's all coming apart," I whisper back but, as soon as we enter the chambers, Artur grabs one from a rack of robes and slips into it.

"Phew," says Loie.

The judge enters the room and everyone stands. The silence is broken as Loie, whispering so softly now that I can barely make it out, tells me that the judge is a woman and that she is putting a curly white wig over her blonde hair. Katarzyna says something to the judge, probably about my blindness, and then the judge proceeds to ask me questions in Polish which Katarzyna translates. My replies, transmitted via Katarzyna, are then repeated by the judge to a court recorder on the judge's left: the year of my birth, our arrival in America, the name of the boat, the year of our naturalization, the years of each of my parents' deaths in New York. I confirm that Paulina was my grandmother, Solomon my grandfather, Stanislaw my uncle—all the judge wants to know to prove that Edward Prokocimer, my Prokocimer grandmother's nephew, lied to a Polish court in 1946; the information is needed to clear the way to my wresting the Stradomska tenement from its wrongful owners. After a half hour, we are dismissed but required to appear the following day before the same judge but in different chambers, where she asks me pretty much the same questions.

"Why this second time?" I ask Artur as we make our way out of the building.

Shrugging his shoulders, he smiles. "This is Po-po-po-land," is all he says and, as he drives us back in his Mercedes

SL500, Artur tells us about a beachfront property he bought in Zanzibar. Who is this guy? Does he really care about this slum property? Why is he even bothering? Surely he hasn't made all his money pursuing little jobs like this one. "Jesus, Loie, this whole thing is beginning to smell bad," I say as we step into the hotel lobby.

"Don't start worrying yet," she advises as we wait for the elevator.

"Loie, do we really want this property?" Inside our room she sits down to rest. "What am I doing joining lawyers and bureaucrats? It's all about money. There is something loathsome about it."

Late that night, I conjure up my grandparents again. My grandmother is smiling. Her face is round, lined but beautiful. I ask her if she and Solomon were on guard when they walked in the streets. "Did you trust the people in the shops? Did you smile? Did you have Polish friends you could trust?"

"Oh yes," she tells me, sitting up straight. "We had a few friends who were not Jewish. I must admit that it was more comfortable being with Jews than the others but it certainly had nothing to do with religion."

"We weren't very Jewish ourselves," my grandfather adds.

"Were you angry? Did you hate?"

"People are not all good," Paulina admits, "but there were bad Jews as well as bad Poles."

"But the Poles hated you because you were Jewish," I proclaim. "Knowing this makes me hate these people." I swallow hard. "Surely you don't forgive them."

"It's better not to spoil your time on earth by hating," she scolds gently. "It makes for a bad appetite."

Okay, she's right. I change the subject. "My father, your son, never told me a joke," I complain, having no idea where this will lead.

"Your father was a sick man," my grandmother says. "Even when he was small, he liked to be alone. He was not happy. He liked staring out the window at nothing."

"But you, what jokes you must have known, stories you must have told."

"So Moishe and Shlomo who had been riding in the same street car after work for many years finally speak," my grandfather says. "'Every day for over twenty years we meet and never say a word,' Moishe says. 'Let's have a conversation. Let's get to know one another.' So Shlomo says, 'What a fine idea, and about time. So tell me my friend, how is your health?' And Moishe says, 'Don't ask, don't ask.'"

3.

The next day, having performed our duty testifying, we wait at the Hotel Rubinstein bar for Artur or Basia to drive us to the Krakow airport. "By the way," Loie says, "Basia told me that younger generations are not nearly as anti-Semitic as the old folks. Only in rural areas do vestiges of old hatreds remain."

The young, charming bartender asks us how we slept last night, reporting that there was a party of noisy Jews on our floor. "Jews? How do you know they were Jews?" I ask her.

She says nothing for a moment, wondering, I am sure, why this question. She smiles, moves closer to me. "Jewish noise," she whispers and offers to pour me a daytime vodka.

"Tell me, Jadzia, how is Jewish noise different from Polish noise?"

She seems unperturbed. I have no idea what's going on in her mind. She smiles and tells me about the klezmer band that sometimes plays a few blocks down the street.

"Do you like that awful music, Mr. Andrew?" I tell her that I like it and she steps back a little, takes a deep breath. "You are Jewish, Mr. Andrew?" she asks.

"I am Jewish," I tell her, hating to use the Polish word for Jew, its sound ugly, accusatory.

Loie does not translate this into anti-Semitism and I suspect that she is right. Jewish noise? I've had reactions like that inside a loud Jewish deli in New York. Also, truth to tell, I'm not all that fond of klezmer music either, though I'm defending it as if it defined me. My over the top sensitivity to Jew hatred appears every time I step into the land of my birth. If I lived here, I would have learned by now to shrug this off as simply part of the language, a low-grade virus that won't go away. Although I am quite bored with enshrined political correctness, I have been thoroughly sensitized by America liberalism to anything remotely smelling of racism. I hate racism everywhere and, for a sobering moment, I realize that, in my anti-racist zeal, I could be accused of it at moments such as this, pinning a label on poor Jadzia, the Hotel Rubinstein bartender, who would probably be shocked and insulted if she thought anyone considered her anti-Semitic. Though it might be true that this younger Polish generation has shed blatant Jew hatred, I can't help wondering if its remnants are stored in some part of the amygdala which, among its various capabilities, must have a special corner reserved for racial memory. I wonder whether every Polish Jew revisiting his place of birth is as supersensitive as I am to even an unexpressed anti-Semitism. Is he, like me, liable to erupt at a moment's notice, a kind of cellular reaction, antibodies lined up to fight infection?

It is Basia in her little Fiat Polonez, not Artur, who drives us to a small airport not far from the center of the city. "The only way Artur could get you back to the States Friday is on Air Berlin," she tells us.

"Shit," I say to Loie. "What a way to end this week." After saying good-bye, we are subjected to that language which, even in the dulcet tones of the flight attendant, puts me on edge. The thought of Mozart or Schubert speaking this harsh and jarring German is disturbing. I prefer Polish.

PART TWO

9

BACK HOME

1.

A few days after we get back to Vermont, I have a dream. Walking along a rocky beach, I'm surprised by an incoming tide. Little by little the water rises to my ankles and I start backing up toward the cliffs that loom above the beach. The ocean does not stop rising and I climb higher. There is no time to dawdle and I grab rock after rock, the water outracing me, now up to my knees. It doesn't let up. I'm breathing hard but keep climbing. With the water at my waist, I reach a ledge, an outcrop of land, and a little boy appears. He begins dancing around me, clapping his hands, cheering me on. "You can do it, you can do it," he sings, and I recognize him. He is the eight-year-old me and I awake, smiling.

A month later, Anita calls to remind me that it is the nineteenth of April, the seventieth anniversary of the Warsaw Ghetto Uprising. On that day long ago, hundreds of adults and children, sparsely armed with handguns and gasoline bottles, had had enough and were ready to fight. Surely they did not view their actions as an effective way to save themselves or to inflict the kind of damage that must have filled their wild revenge dreams. It was a battle for the honor of the Jewish people, and a protest against the world's silence. The uprising was the largest single revolt by Jews in the war, and it ended when the poorly armed and supplied resistance was crushed by the Germans, who officially finished their operation to liquidate the ghetto on May 16, razing every building within it and blowing up the Great Synagogue.

By coincidence, a conference began in Bermuda on the first day of the uprising, in which the Allied powers decided that saving the Jews would prolong the war and damage the war effort. Thus US immigration quotas were not raised, nor was the British prohibition on Jewish refugees seeking refuge in their Palestine Mandate lifted. I wonder if the delegates to the conference smiled, recognizing that it was only Jews, those pestilent Jews. I assume that cocktails were served after their decision, but in London a member of the Jewish advisory group to the wartime Polish government-in-exile committed suicide in protest.

2.

Basia sends me a copy of her e-mail to Philippe Prokocimer, a nephew of the perpetrator, Edward.

"I am contacting you on behalf of Mr. Bobrowski, who represents Mr. Andrew Potok, your cousin from Vermont," she wrote. "Let me draft a brief historical background, so that everything sounds logical. The property was owned (before the WWII) half and half by two brothers, namely Szewah and Abe vel Abbe Prokocimer (your great-grandfather). Szewah's daughter, Rosa Saphier, sold half of the property after WWII to a Polish family. After your great-grandparents' . . . death but still before the war, the other half went to your grandfather, Wolf Wilhelm, and his five siblings, including the grandmother—Paulina Potok née Prokocimer—of our client.

"In 1946 your uncle, Edward Prokocimer, testified before the court in Krakow that he was the sole survivor of the Prokocimer family. He even concealed the existence of his own brother—Bruno, your father. That is how Edward came into half of the property, while, lawfully, he should have acquired a one-eighth interest, and your father, Bruno, also a one-eighth interest. Sons of Paulina Potok—Leon Potok (father of our client) and his brother Stanislaw Potok (who died childless in the UK in 1984)—should also have received a one-eighth interest each. According to the current status of the property, half of the tenement is titled to Edward's son, Marian [aka Miron], and Edward's wife, Helena, who are residing in Israel.

"On behalf of our client and your cousin, Andrew Potok, we have filed a petition for reversing the 1946 court's decision, under which Edward Prokocimer received your grandfather's [Wolf's] interest. . . . On request of the court, Mr. Potok came to Krakow in order to testify the truth. After the hearing, the court have requested and obligated us to present all information of and contact details to Bruno Prokocimer and, in case he is not alive, to his natural heirs, namely to you and to your siblings. Since it is neither known, nor confirmed, if your father is alive, he is represented (in all proceedings) by a delegated custodian. . . .

"We know from experience that no-one is ever willing to return assets worth circa 2,2 million PLN—according to the today's currency exchange rate, approximately $600–700,000. (One-eighth interest would be worth at least $150–180,000.) We expect, therefore, Marian Prokocimer to try to contest the petition, though we believe this may only generate additional costs for him, because if he loses, he will have to cover all court's fees and expenses."

Even though my grandmother Paulina was a Prokocimer before she married Solomon Potok, I knew little about the Prokocimers until now. As a result of Basia's e-mail, Philippe Prokocimer calls me from his office in San Diego. To my surprise, he seems to know nothing about the Krakow property. "Your father Bruno never mentioned it?" I ask.

"Nothing at all," he says with a captivating French accent. I ask if he knows his cousin Miron (Marian) Prokocimer in Israel. "Just a little," he says. "My brother Didier, sister Beatrice, and I are born in Paris where my father Bronek—that is his Polish name—settled and where he lived during the war years. But tell me, Andrew—I may call you Andrew?" he asks. "After all we are cousins." I assure him that he can call me Andrew. "It is my uncle Edward who takes the whole property?" he asks.

"That is what I understand."

"This is difficult to believe," he says, "but I am going to Paris to visit my family in a month and will ask them what they think of this whole business." He gives me several phone numbers where he can be reached and the best times to call. "You must keep in touch," he says. Philippe is the chief medical officer of Trius Therapeutics in San Diego and, according to Basia, earns a huge salary, making me question how much attention he will pay to the recovery of a tenement in Poland not only because, to him, the amount might be financially insignificant, but also because of the bother of being forced to appear in Polish court and the possible sowing of family feuds.

My contact with a Prokocimer gives me no special sense of family, a similar feeling to the emptiness I experienced when Anita and I found no remnants of a house in Wieliszew, the locus of my transformation from innocent child to battered, untrusting, and empty little body . . .

After hanging up the phone, I sit at my desk and day-dream Paulina into existence. "I need to know so many things from you," I whisper. "Did you ever live in that apartment house on Stradomska? You can be sure that you wouldn't want to live inside those walls today." Paulina says nothing but I go on. "What did you think of your nephew Edward?" There is something more that I should know about this man who, a year after the war ended, lied about an ugly building and stole Stradomska Thirteen from the rest of the family. I'm wondering what I would have done in the Poland of 1946? Edward Prokocimer's betrayal may have been the only way he could have saved himself. How to judge any action taken seventy years ago in the chaos of post-war Poland? The nation was destroyed and depleted, more than three million Poles and the same number of Jews slaughtered. When Edward Prokocimer swore to the Polish court that he was the family's sole survivor, he could have been dazed or driven mad by whatever he experienced during the war. Though I know nothing about him or his life, no one survived without deep scars. I imagine myself standing in front of some Polish judge, not knowing if I could trust him to be fair, not knowing if he had collaborated with the Germans or joined resistance fighters in the woods. If I had lived through the war in Europe as I suppose Edward did, and stood in front of a Polish judge, I'm not at all sure if I would have bothered to think of who else was alive. "Did you call him Edek or Edzio?" I ask my grandmother. "Can you believe that he betrayed his brother Bronek and your children, my father Leon and uncle Stash?" The silence of time pulls me into its impenetrability, as nightmarish as the huge blackness that once inhabited my dreams. I think I am losing my mind as the list of impenetrables overwhelms me. "Did you even know you had a heritable disease?" She doesn't speak. "I am blind from it," I tell her and still not a sound.

3.

Thousands of miles from the vanished Warsaw Ghetto, I sit at my computer during another Vermont mud season, and listen to an article from the day's *New York Times*, which describes the nearly finished Museum of Jewish History being constructed on the site of the former ghetto. The article distinguishes between present guilt regarding anti-Semitism in Germany and in Poland. Though German society has accepted collective guilt for the genocide of European Jews, Poles consider themselves equally victimized and do not accept their role as happy onlookers and sometimes active participants. In researching the article, the *Times*'s Nicholas Kulish interviewed 1,250 Warsaw high school students and asked them who, in their opinion, suffered more in the war, Jews or Poles, and nearly half answered that they suffered equally. What if they found out that a boyfriend or girlfriend was Jewish or if they discovered that there was a Jew in their family? Well over half said they would be unhappy. Ironically, the numbers were similar when Israeli high school students were asked the same question regarding Arabs.

Probably I am one of the few readers of the *New York Times* article who doesn't respond to the building of the museum with a sigh of relief and hope for a better future. Building the museum, financed mainly by American Jews, seems a better idea than not building it. Because of the new structure, Poles have at least stopped denying the impact of Jews on Polish history during the thousand years of cohabitation. However, with very few Jews living in Poland, this acknowledgement no longer threatens Polish identity as it would have in the past.

At times, I do allow myself a more moderate view: poor Poland. What a tragedy to be plunked between barbaric Germany and barbaric Russia, between Hitler and Stalin, or to be neighbors of the Ukraine, Belarus, Lithuania, Estonia, and Latvia, Jew killers all. After all, at the end of the eighteenth century Poland was carved up and occupied by the Russian Empire, by the Kingdom of Prussia, and by the Austrian Hapsburg Monarchy, not becoming Poland again until the end of World War I, and that for only twenty years. And during World War II, there was less Polish collaboration and the most active resistance of any of the occupied countries of Europe. Still, the so-called Home Army and the many partisans in the forests did not welcome the Jewish fighters who wanted to join them. Not only did they not want Jews to participate in the guerilla action, but these brave defenders of Poland often killed the Jews who tried to participate in ridding the country of its German occupiers. In fact, during the occupation, Poles killed more Jews than the Germans did.

The immediate post–World War II years were a period of social upheaval on a monumental scale. More than a million Poles were repatriated by the end of 1946 from the Ukraine, Lithuania, and Belorussia, while another quarter million returned from the Soviet interior, more than half of them Polish Jews. The huge movement of peoples had been decided by Churchill, Roosevelt, and Stalin at the conferences of Tehran in 1943 and Potsdam in 1945, with similar unforeseen consequences to the nations involved, just as the Allied decisions that followed World War I to create new borders, even new nations, led to enormous brutality and loss of life. In Tehran, Churchill proposed to move the western parts of Poland farther west into industrial German lands while ceding much of Poland's eastern land to the Soviet Union, providing a territorial buffer against invasion to the delighted Stalin. In Potsdam, the Western powers agreed to Soviet control of Poland, a terrible unjust sellout from the Polish point of view, offering them as an unearned prize to the Communists and condemning them to another more-than-forty years of brutal occupation.

The post-war fate of that part of the world, after unimagined years of bloodthirsty behavior, combined an ugly nationalist fervor with an atmosphere of chaos and hunger for vengeance. The Ukrainians set upon the Poles, the Poles upon the Ukrainians as well as the Germans who had lived for many generations on land now given to Poland as a kind of reparation. The Polish Jews who had repatriated from areas of the Soviet Union were greeted by pent-up hostility; many were murdered as Soviet sympathizers or simply for trying to reclaim their abandoned homes.

By 1946, 500,000 Soviet troops were stationed in Poland. Some 150,000 Poles, including prominent leaders of the Polish wartime underground, were imprisoned, and all opposition parties were banned. Nevertheless, there was plenty of venom left in the Polish heart, enough to sponsor little pogroms in Krakow and elsewhere, including the big one in the town of Kielce.

4.

I saddle up my Gabriel and we slosh our way to a coffee shop in town where I sit surrounded by cheerful Vermonters. At least for now, this Polish business won't let go. Apartness and aloneness won't loosen their grip on me. I'm like a zombie amid talk of weather and last night's episode of *Modern Family*. And here I sit, recalling a Jewish survivor of the Warsaw Ghetto Uprising saying, "The Germans, they shot you, that's all. The Poles murdered you with axes. Poland is probably the only country in the world where practically the whole society betrayed and handed over to the Germans each hidden Jew, their fellow citizens. Thousands of Jewish children were caught this way, handed over to the Germans and sent on to the gas chambers. The entire

Polish society is to be blamed, and the Polish clergy most of all."

A book I am reading, *Neighbors*, by Jan Gross, describes an incident that took place in July 1941. Jews had lived in the town of Jedwabne since 1660. At the end of the nineteenth century, they made up eighty percent of the town's population. By the start of World War II, the balance of ethnic Poles and Jews was more or less equal. After two years of German occupation, half the population of Jedwabne murdered the other half, the Jewish half, an estimated 1,600 men, women, and children.

The massacre began on the morning of July 10, 1941, when eight Gestapo members arrived and had a meeting with town authorities. When the Gestapo asked what their plans were with respect to the Jews, the Poles responded unanimously, saying that all Jews must be killed. When the Germans proposed to leave one Jewish family from each profession, local carpenter Bronislaw Sleszyliski answered, "We have enough of our own craftsmen, we have to destroy all the Jews, none should stay alive." Mayor Karolak and the others agreed with his words.

Among the killers, mostly small farmers and seasonal workers, were two shoemakers, a mason, a carpenter, two locksmiths, a letter carrier, and a former town hall receptionist. Some had children, some not. The youngest was twenty-seven years old, the oldest sixty-four. They armed themselves with axes and special clubs studded with nails, and chased all the Jews into the street. They selected seventy-five of the youngest and healthiest Jews, whom they ordered to pick up a huge monument of Lenin that the Russians had erected in the center of town. While carrying the monument, they were forced to sing until they brought it to the designated place. There, they were ordered to dig a hole and throw the monument in. Then they were killed and thrown into the same hole. Beards of old Jews were burned, newborn babies were killed at their mothers' breasts, people were beaten and forced to sing and dance. In the end they proceeded to the main attraction, a barn donated for this purpose by a farmer named Sleszpiski, in front of which Jews were forced to line up in a column, four in a row, the ninety-year-old rabbi and the Kosher butcher put in front, then beaten and ordered to sing as they were herded into the barn which, with its exits secured, was doused with kerosene and lit. All the town's Jews inside the barn were burned alive.

The deed done, the townspeople searched Jewish homes for anyone who was left behind. The sick and the children were carried to the barn and thrown onto smoldering coals. And that was that. By the time the sun set, the task was completed and everyone went back home for the evening meal.

For those who say that 1941 was a long time ago and that the butchery happened during a brutal German occupation, and claim that since the war Poland has changed, the story of Jedwabne has not yet ended. In Anna Bikont's monumental book *The Crime and the Silence*, she writes that a monument to the Jews killed in 1941 was erected in Jedwabne in 2001 as a reminder of what took place there. This monument has been vandalized and covered with swastikas. People on the street still maintain that when old Jewish men, women, and children did not fight back against those Polish men who beat them with guns and clubs, those Jews deserved their fate. To be burned alive. Now, the Poles of Jedwabne maintain that if Jews seek to uncover exactly what happened in July 1941, it is another sign of their historic greed for gold, not of their desire to learn the truth. Thus the Jews are seen as ruining Poland's reputation as a country of honorable Christian people. In fact, copies of *The Protocols of the Elders of Zion* are still being distributed outside the church at Jedwabne.

How can the argument that Poland is not a special case in the world of hate, of anti-Semitism, be made in light of Polish denial to this day that Poles were not responsible for the deaths of Jedwabne's Jews? It is not only in rural Poland where it is still dangerous to blame Poles. Reading Anna Bikont's book, how can one not acknowledge her bravery in facing the anti-Semites while traveling throughout Poland for research purposes? In Warsaw, where she lives, her newspaper is inundated with denials. It doesn't sound all that different from pre-war times when the most assimilated Jews, my family among them, suffered constant indignities in the streets, shops, and restaurants. The Polish nation, wrapped in its primitive Catholicism, seems unable to stop defending itself from victims or commentators regarding its history of hatred, which is cited on every page of *The Crime and the Silence*. It's not easy to accept Polish failure to admit complicity; they deny their own guilt so as to preserve a false national pride, often accompanied by professions of faith in some higher morality. Even that Solidarity hero and Nobel Peace Prize recipient, Lech Walesa, when asked for comment about Jan Gross's book, *Neighbors*, said, "Gross was out to sow discord among Poles and Jews. He is a mediocre writer, a Jew who tries to make money."

The cancer that is Polish anti-Semitism stems from the country's self-image as "the martyr of Europe, the Christ among nations." When I visited Auschwitz in 1979, the place was considered a symbol of Polish martyrdom. Celebrated in Auschwitz's annals of victimhood, though a horror in its own right, were 74,000 Poles, 21,000 Roma, 15,000 Soviet prisoners of war, and 12,000 from all other nations. The million Jews gassed there were considered a peripheral, trivial matter.

5.

It isn't much fun to be with me these days, especially for Loie who would welcome a bit of cheerfulness in the house. But where to find it? I poke around the Internet and find Mel Brooks and Anne Bancroft singing "Sweet Georgia Brown" in Polish, an act I have always cherished, then Lennie Bruce, Tom Lehrer, Jonathan Winters, old stuff, my stuff, but I need more. Mort Sahl, Shelly Berman, Woody Allen. I try reading Mark Twain. All of it helps, but I can't shake being more attuned to the world's disasters, its racism and classism, its pernicious violence and hatreds. I am mired in memoirs of Auschwitz, histories of slaughters, the struggles of all minorities, and I wonder if Jews are any more hated than, say, the Chinese by the Japanese or vice versa, more than Mexicans by Americans, Tutsis by Hutus, Shia by Sunni, Catholics by Protestants, one stupid belief system versus another. Because tribes were threatened by neighbors in the Pleistocene, are we forever genetically predestined to carry human hatred toward anyone not a member of our own tribe? Are we bound to forever protect, mistrust, kill?

At times, I not only hate those who lust for power—the anti-Semites, the Tea Party, and the one percent—but, being the armchair hater and freedom fighter, a paper tiger, no threat to anyone, I hate most, not all, singer-songwriters— not knowing Joni Mitchell from Joanie of Arc—all Irish music, French-Canadian music, military drum rolls, national anthems, accordions, harmonicas, Andre Bocelli— all kitsch, lukewarm on the palate, repeating themselves ad nauseam.

William Hazlitt wrote one of my favorite essays, "On the Pleasure of Hating." "Without something to hate, we should lose the very spring of thought and action. Life would turn to a stagnant pool, were it not ruffled by the jarring interests, the unruly passions, of men. The white streak in our own fortunes is brightened (or just rendered visible) by making all around it as dark as possible."

"You have to learn not to hate," Loie says, always the moderate one, the normalizer who needs to pluck things out of craziness. I know intellectually that there is an obverse side to rage and depression. I know that they do not have to dominate my life, but I don't know if I'll ever be capable of minimizing or neutralizing the war criminals or racists, the believers in astrology and angels. I must transform "may they die" or "stand them up against the wall" into generosity and compassion. Even knowing that anger might be a dead end, probably not a contributor to longevity, I fear that without it, I would lose my identity. "You can re-story your identity," Loie says sweetly. "Anger isn't the most attractive identity."

At the beginning of the eighth century, an Indian Buddhist named Shantideva wrote, "All the virtuous deeds and merit, such as giving and making offerings, that we have accumulated can be destroyed by just one moment of anger." Hmmm, maybe. He goes on to write, "There is no evil greater than anger, and no virtue greater than patience. If I harbour painful thoughts of anger, I shall not experience mental peace, I shall find no joy or happiness, and I shall be unsettled and unable to sleep." You betcha, Shantideva.

From Aristotle to Martha Nussbaum, philosophers have given anger a bad name, but anger has its healthy sides. It's on a different moral scale than a wish for payback or violent retribution, though sometimes it leads to private fantasies such as mine: imagining a bit of German soil being ceded to survivors of death camps. But just as acceptance of the reality of despicable human behavior is, in my mind, far better than forgiveness, anger is a more honest and heartfelt response to injustice, intolerance, greed, or corruption than a meek turning of the other cheek.

Though art has hardly ever changed the course of history—art being largely a conversation between the artist and the viewer or listener or reader—when we look for solace from having been bruised by the world situation and we feel impotent after joining a movement, going to meetings, or calling a legislator, a committed artist will make art, an angry art that tries to spark a larger conversation, one about fear and hatred, about racism, torture, and greed.

In America, the righteous rage of black people regarding their continued oppression would be well served by reparations, not retribution, that would legally assure black populations a first-rate education, top of the line health care, and an end to redlining housing, with a non-racist government's assurance that interference or negligence would be punishable by strictly enforced law. The new society, just and principled, would go a long way to right the wrongs inflicted for hundreds of years of slavery, plus many more years of racism, legal and illegal, the inhumanity of which has deprived generations of equal opportunity. This is not payback or retribution. It would punish no one, though it might hurt the feelings of racists and realtors. Serious racist criminals of any nation should be confined to institutions, either for possible rehabilitation or, if faced with irremediable criminality, locked up for as long as it takes. Truth and reconciliation commissions have been noble attempts at dealing humanely with perpetrators—a little truth not a bad idea in identifying war criminals in several American administrations as it has in South African ones—but allowing war criminals, predatory bankers, racist police, ignorant avengers, rapists, slayers of innocents to go unpunished is dangerously anti-social, deterring the construction and maintenance of a humane society.

For the most part, we torture and kill only under orders from elderly heads of state pursuing glory and power, or because of religious dogma, intent on preserving and protecting its claim to speak for the really, really true God. Functionaries and bureaucrats, as well as priests and Imams, whether German, Polish, or Russian, whether Saudi, Egyptian, or American, justify mass murders in the name of ideology, profane or sacred. It is clear to me that this phenomenon applies not only to the Hans Franks or Eichmanns of the world but to the corporate heads of insurance companies who deny coverage to the sick; to bailed-out bankers who, while amassing enormous fortunes, force people out of homes, not unlike the cautious eighteenth-century bookkeepers in Liverpool who had no trouble simply noting the profits and losses from the Atlantic slave trade in their tidy ledgers. They all kill with impunity, and whether they do so out of stupidity or thoughtlessness or for pleasure makes little difference to their victims.

When I momentarily abandon anger, I can even admit a possibility of hope regarding that newly erected Museum of Jewish History in Warsaw whose usefulness in the eradication of Polish anti-Semitism I doubted. If all Polish school children are required to visit the museum at least once, that might not be a total solution to the problem of anti-Semitism but, once free of the anti-Semitism of their parents, children might indeed begin to question all hatred.

6.

When I fall into depression and negativity, when I become a joyless, energyless person and Loie no longer wants anything to do with me, I begin all over again to think of myself as the son of Leon—Leon Potok, my father. Loving and being loved by women, being desired, has always separated me from him. At those times when I am not wanted, I become him.

Having listened to clients all day long, Loie comes home from work tired from empathizing, taking on others' miseries. At the end of my workday, I too am exhausted but, having spent the day alone with my thoughts, I need conversation. She does not relish my eagerness to talk, prompting me once again to suspect that I am living my father's life. When my mother came home exhausted from shlepping all day, fitting seal and mink and sable onto a Kennedy or the Duke and Duchess of Windsor, she did not like being with my depressed father. I wonder if he wanted to kill her. To steal all her money, hers and Max's, to set that fucking Maximilian Furs on fire. At the end of the workday when my brain feels like oatmeal, I look forward to a martini and perhaps a glass of wine with dinner. My father did not allow himself any such pleasure.

Since our return from Poland, in relatively harmless Vermont, Loie, together with a few young poets and dancers, has created a program intended to stress individual differences and encourage empathy in classrooms of kids of all ages. "Six-, seven-, and eight-year-olds put their unwanted negative feelings into spider-web boxes," she tells me, "and they're able to confront and transform their negative feelings, angers, hatreds, revenge fantasies, into positive useful ones. Kids can still do it with ease," Loie says. "If only they would do something like this in Poland," she adds.

In spite of Loie's activism in the prevention of hatreds toward any "other," I continue to torture myself by reading about Poles who dug up the fields around Treblinka and other burial pits, looking for gold to extract from the teeth of buried Jewish skulls, then protecting their dug-up treasure from their neighbors who, they knew, would kill for the gold. Anyone in Poland who sheltered Jews during the war faced a German death sentence but, if not discovered by the occupiers, they not only had to protect themselves from their friends and neighbors who hungered for the stolen Jewish gold but had to fear being stigmatized as "Jew lovers."

I try to rationalize these acts. Poverty? Pure ignorance? Lack of a gene or two that might promote morality? If these were families with children, did their children help? If they confessed to their priests, did a few Hail Marys wipe the slate clean or did the priests join in the search?

A man testifying about the activities of the church during the war wrote that priests often discussed the Jews in church and thanked God that these parasites were gone once and for all. Adam Chetnik, a distinguished Polish ethnographer, noted in his diary in 1941: "In Warsaw one does not see Jews anymore, and some say that it would be hard to get used to them once again. In any case, we do not feel their absence."

I know I have to stop broadcasting my feelings. No one seems eager to be with me and none of it is helping dissipate the gloom at home.

7.

Some of my friends deny that Polish anti-Semitism is special and think it should not be the cause of obloquy. To them, Claude Lanzmann's film *Shoah* is unfair in singling out Poland as the prime malefactor. I assume that their objection to Lanzmann comes from their respect and admiration for those Poles who were not Jew haters, those who put their own lives on the line by protecting Jews. And indeed, according to Yad Vashem's count, there were six thousand Poles, more than from any other nation, among the righteous, those who considered all humans as equals.

Cultural and intellectual life in Poland has always been lively, often extraordinary. Assuming that no trace of post-Enlightenment piety or unswerving devotion to the somewhat discredited Polish church still exists among them, a few recent examples of the many I admire are philosophers such as Leszek Kolakowski, composers such as Krzysztof

Panderecki, poets such as Czeslaw Milosz, Zbygniew Herbert, and Wyslawa Szymborska.

Since returning from Krakow, I've been listening to every book, recorded or scanned into my computer, regarding anti-Semitism, Jewishness, Christianity, Polish history, the many aspects of evil. The hard, cold winter in north central Vermont has not contributed much gaiety to the somber, though enlightening, subject matter.

One morning at breakfast with two good friends, we talk of old times, the Bread and Puppet Circus settling nearby, the quixotic history of Goddard College, the state of our wood piles. Knowing my current obsession with Poland and "the Jewish question," they mention a book they think I should read, a memoir in the guise of a novel, *Fatelessness*, by Imre Kertesz, the great Hungarian writer and Nobel Prize winner sent to Auschwitz and Buchenwald when he was fourteen years old. Because I am only a year younger than Kertesz, the horrors of his experience strike close to home. In 1944, when he was picked up in the streets of Budapest in the huge Eichmann deportations before the end of the war, I was thirteen, safely tucked away in a New England school. Kertesz's memories of being pulled out of the cattle car onto the famous selection platform in Auschwitz, and his excitement encountering German troops in their splendid warlike uniforms, was not like anything I had read before. At fourteen, he was intrigued and curious rather than fearful. But then, transported from Auschwitz to Buchenwald, he barely survived the subsequent year of torture. Never, before *Fatelessness*, could I imagine myself as a child or a teenager experiencing those initial moments as adventure. It seemed possible that, like Kertesz, I might have done so, before experiencing the horror the death camp turned out to be.

In Kertesz's Nobel acceptance speech he said, "The existential labor that being an Auschwitz-survivor has thrust upon me is a kind of obligation. I realize what a privilege has been bestowed on me. I have seen the true visage of this dreadful century, I have gazed into the eye of the Gorgon, and have been able to keep on living. Yet, I knew I would never be able to free myself from the sight; I knew this visage would always hold me captive . . . I have never succumbed to the temptation of self-pity, nor, it may be, to that of true sublimity and divine perspicacity, but I have known from the beginning that my disgrace was not merely a humiliation; it also concealed redemption, if only my heart could be courageous enough to accept this redemption, this peculiarly cruel form of grace, and even to recognize grace at all in such a cruel form. And if you now ask me what still keeps me here on this earth, what keeps me alive, then, I would answer without any hesitation: love."

Love? As I first read his words, I have to re-read this passage, but there it is again. Love. Tears are streaming down my cheeks. I don't know what this really means, how Auschwitz leads to love. My little traumas of the time were not even flesh wounds compared with the unimaginable horrors of Kertesz's mid-teens, but he emerged with redemption, grace, and love. I emerged with numbness. Of course, as a child, I didn't make that choice. My body did. Different bodies make different choices and take different roads for the remainder of their lives. I don't even know how to learn from Kertesz. I can only stand to one side, take a deep breath, and experience an incomprehensible awe.

Now, with the reawakening of my Polish years, numbness is no longer an option. I suppose that, as I numbed out the trauma, I could have become a sociopath, a killer, a warrior, a nasty cop, a seeker of absolute truths, a monk, an ideologue for whom the end justified any means. Posttrauma, people have been known to turn to anti-social rebellion, thuggery and murder and suicide. I could also have learned to forgive, to become a hermit, a leader. There seems to be no pattern in the lives of refugees, of the traumatized, the badly parented.

So here I am in progressive Vermont, comfortable, well taken care of and caring, blind but not yet dying of some dread disease, the trees budding I am told, the climate temperate, spring upon us. I am in the throes of unresolved pain, not caused by some virulent act of Jew hatred or by personal affronts, and yet I feel like a knight in armor, Don Quixote, prepared to slash and pierce, ready for the hint of a slur. No real estate is worth the state of mind this pursuit of property recovery has produced, not to mention the expenditure of time and intense emotion. I cannot stop trying to understand the terror that once gripped me, succeeded by the terror that remained in my thinking about the world. I wish I could connect it to my painting, my deep love of music, to the way I deal with blindness, my ability to love and, too often, the ease with which I lapse into anger and hatred. Terror tends to poison all love, generosity, and compassion as inconspicuously as a brown recluse spider crawled into Loie's suitcase in California and bit her cheek when she unpacked in Vermont. I know that hatred accomplishes nothing except to poison the hater. Unfortunately, forgiveness is not my answer. No philosophy of goodness could entice me to forgive. I am told that forgiving costs nothing. Not true. Whether forgiveness is demanded by some cockamamie religious belief or simply on the advice of a therapist or, better yet, for the sake of rational self-preservation, it's not easy to surrender a righteous rage if it's a powerful center of self-identity.

If there had been no war, I imagine that I would have been sent to school in England, and perhaps the Apfelbaum's Warsaw business and their Bedzin homes and factories would have continued to exist. The recent trip to Krakow has unleashed what I never before faced with such emotional clarity: rage, which has disturbed the complacent part of my existence. I'm afraid that my days will end with hatred in my heart and, wisdom to the contrary, it's also possible, though unlikely, that the hatred will keep me alive for a long time to come.

The feelings that I am wrestling with are not just about anti-Semitism generally, but about the choices my own family made living within the belly of that beast. They were allowed to live comfortably because of their assimilation, and rewarded with a tacit acceptance by wealthy Poles. The Apfelbaum clan was servile as any good fashion merchant, performing admirably, with humility and generosity, offering Poles and wealthy folks from all over Europe furs beautifully designed by my mother from bundles of pelts bought at Leningrad auctions by Max. But how comfortable could they have been preparing a fashion show at the Hotel Bristol or being led to their table by the maître d' at one of the great Villanova restaurants? Was my mother smiling? Did Max protrude his chest proudly, pigeon-like? Did the waiters grouse in the kitchen about serving those Jews? Did they even feel like Jews? And then, what if our Citroen van had not made it to the Lithuanian border? In rural Poland, not far from the border crossing, the peasant population would have happily stopped plowing their fields, run for their barns where the knives and clubs hung, and cut us up for fertilizer. Were all peasants who worked the land capable of such brutality? Are they still? If one can slaughter animals for food, does it make the slaughter of fellow humans easier? What if we had turned back to Warsaw? Even with my family's connections to the rulers of the place, it seems unlikely that any of us would have survived the German hatred of Jews. Most of the family who stayed behind were equally assimilated, which didn't prevent their murder by German men or the takeover of their apartments and possessions by unquenchable human thirst. And we would have been pushed into the ghetto and from there to Treblinka or Auschwitz. But none of this happened to me or my parents or Anita or Max or Zosia.

A friend sent me electronically an unpublished memoir by a survivor who, because of ingenious stealth and unbelievable luck, made it through the war in Poland. He was my age when the war started but was surely made of sterner stuff. Though also the son of merchants, he and his family lived in the Warsaw Ghetto, whereas my parents and I lived in the thick of a Christian community. Thoughtful, even scholarly, his story of seemingly random decisions, uncanny, unimaginable escapes, though surely true, are too unbelievable for even a bad movie. When he was twelve, he joined other child smugglers outside the ghetto walls, and when the ghetto uprising began, he managed to flee to the countryside where he worked on a farm, then lived in an orphanage run by the Silesian fathers, constantly fearing that his circumcised penis would be detected. After he spent the entire war hiding out from Germans and Poles, all but a very few of the latter eager to turn him in, much to my amazement he wrote that it was unjust to condemn a whole nation on the basis of the behavior of a few. A few? Which Poland was he referring to? Though he could not have been aware then of Jedwabne or Kielce or any of the many other places in the country where "neighbors" slaughtered Jews during and after the war, he must know better by now. A few Poles did have a hand in his survival, but Jew hatred, collaboration, the pleasure he must have seen on their faces as the Jews disappeared, was in the air he breathed. His father, who had bought the birth certificate of a Christian child murdered in a concentration camp, intended to help his son survive as a Pole, but someone discovered that one of the murdered child's parents was Jewish, putting the memoirist's life in mortal danger again, especially were his circumcised penis to be detected. Because of his ability to forgive, he is probably living a happier life after the war than he would have if he had carried hatred in his heart, but it is beyond me to imagine the fortitude, the denial or charity, it took to let it go, to accept evil. It surpasses any of my attempts to understand it.

In his Nobel acceptance speech, Kertesz said that most efforts to bring the Holocaust to people's consciousness have been sentimental at best. Referring to Spielberg's movie *Schindler's List*, Kertesz said, "I regard as kitsch any representation of the Holocaust that is incapable of understanding or unwilling to understand the organic connection between our own deformed mode of life and the very possibility of the Holocaust." What he discovered in Auschwitz he describes as "the human condition, the end point of a great adventure, where the European traveler arrived, in the Christian cultural environment, after his two-thousand-year-old moral and cultural history."

10

NATURE AND NURTURE

1.

My psychopharmacologist prescribes a new anti-depressant, adding norepinephrine and dopamine to the serotonin reuptake inhibitors. Like idiots the world over, I want a magic bullet to rocket me out of my misery. The new drug cocktail and a martini, plus the passage of time, might help me get on with my life.

I used to talk weekly on the phone with a New York psychoanalyst who was not only a German Jewish refugee, a few years older than I, but blind. I loved the man. But recently, as dear Norbert was emptying the garbage outside the back door of his West End Avenue apartment, he fell down the back stairs and died, a terrible loss. If only he was there now and I could tell him about Poland, about my anger, about all the pain those memories bring. "I probably shouldn't hate so much," I might have told him, "but I can't get over my hatred."

"Look here," Norbert would have said, "let us call a shpade a shpade. How can you not hate them? It's too easy to forgive." When, at times, I would kvetch about my being a hopeless narcissist, he would say, "Narcissist? Narcissist? Vot is this narcissist? Do not call yourself names."

At home on Richardson Street, I continue my nighttime talks with Paulina and Solomon, seated in front of my slightly open bedroom windows, the cold night air not a problem as I confess my participation in the search for chemicals and every other damn thing to relieve depression, loss of memory, whatever else ails this aging body. "It couldn't have been like this in your time," I say. "None of these nostrums were even invented, crap like Ecstasy, Vicodin, Ritalin, THC, whatever it takes. Some of us scream our hidden kvetches, others repress them. Some eat no sugar or wheat, no animal fat or vegetable oils. Some eat plants grown in sunlight or grown in shade, eat red meat or organic chicken, drink at least two glasses of red wine to keep the blood flowing."

"We loved a glass or two of wine with dinner," my grandmother tells me.

"Nowadays we ask each other, 'How's the urinary tract, the prostate, the knees, the high registers?'" I kvetch, "But above all, we dread the loss of memory. We cannot stop complaining about forgetting a name or a phone number. We make ourselves do crossword puzzles or learn Greek. Some say to forget brain exercise. 'Only physical exercise,' they say. People of all ages sweat to prolong their lives but, to tell the truth, there aren't many my age frolicking or dancing, so we do anything to preserve youth and health."

"And we not?" asks my grandmother. "We ran to the baths, to Carlsbad or Bad Nauheim. We sat in brine and mud. We drank putrid waters that bubbled up through rocks. We closed windows at night to keep bad air away. We wanted to live forever."

"Ah," my grandfather Solomon adds. "Special waters, salt springs bubbling from the ground, good for the heart and nerves."

"The walks in the mountains," Paulina continues, "the beautiful roses, orange ones and yellow and pink."

I am smiling, fortified by thoughts of our familial addiction to seeking help. I turn to my side and, almost asleep, I wish there had been some medication, anything, that might have helped my poor father.

2.

There is no sign yet of the Richardson Street woodpecker. However, the robins are chirping away and other woodpeckers are pecking their hearts out in the woods above us, the Richardson Street dead end sign for now undisturbed.

A week or two into May, Montpelier's streets are torn up for the installation of heavy ducts, which will carry heat from a woodchip burning plant to schools and government buildings, making my walks through town with Gabriel an adventure. On practically every street crossing, sweaty, buff men offer us help. "Would you like to take my arm, sir?" I am flabbergasted by their civility—no pity, just kindness. But bad things happen everywhere. In this lovely New England town, as I stand talking with a friend outside the gym, Gabriel at my side, I hear a beastly snarl and feel Gabriel being pulled away. In his sweet innocence, my dog is being viciously attacked. The perpetrator is on a leash, a woman at its other end. She pulls her dog back and runs. After momentarily examining my poor Gabriel, my friend Nona takes off in pursuit. I run up the stairs into the gym where Gabriel's wound is examined and pronounced serious. I'm down at his side and feel the blood running down his back. He and I are both panting. Nona comes back, out of breath, the hit and run woman nowhere to be found. Someone called Loie and we race to the local vet who performs a long surgery. I call the police who promise to search for the hit-and-run perpetrator but she is never found. Though Gabriel is expected to have psychological repercussions, to slink away from other dogs and refuse to take me back to the scene of the crime, there is no such response from my forgiving dog. After a full recovery, Gabriel seems unaffected by canine PTSD. But it's clear that immorality, at whatever level, has no borders.

In June my son Mark and his wife Carol fly to Poland for an annual international conference attended by some thirty participants, half American, half German, and hosted by the lone Polish member. One year they met in the US, the next in Germany, and now in Warsaw. Their topic and their passion is the outing of hate groups, white supremacists, neo-Nazis, every kind of militia. My son, the editor-in-chief of the Southern Poverty Law Center's *Intelligence Report*, is a hate expert. How strange is that? I the armchair hater, my wonderful firstborn a scholar in the field.

Though very aware of Polish feelings about the Jews before, during, and after the war, both Mark and Carol love being in Poland. Loie and I had been there in miserable weather; now Mark sees it from a totally different perspective, the trees in bloom, the sidewalks gleaming, free of snow and ice.

"Warsaw was beautiful," Mark writes, "the architecture elegant, the shops and restaurants full to capacity, but we really loved Krakow." They stayed in a first-class hotel just off the old Market Square, walked in Kazimierz, and visited a synagogue not far from the Hotel Rubinstein. They traipsed through the ornate interior, abundantly decorated with gold leaf. "We were stopped in our tracks in front of one of the stained glass windows," Mark reports. "In front of us, embedded in the window, appeared the names of Izaak and Amalia Potok 1925."

Izaak and Amalia? I'm amazed that Loie didn't see the window, the two of us having visited the same synagogue a few months before. I also realize that Izaak and Amalia were the parents of my dear Australian cousin Jurek.

When Mark and Carol return from Poland, I fly down to Alabama. As delighted as I am to be with them, I do not like being in the Deep South, to me the Poland of America. Black people continuing to live there seem similar to Jews choosing to stay in Poland, although the two histories are very different. The Southern black experience has included slavery, lynching, and unrelenting American racism, whereas slavery as such has never been a part of European Jewish history.

"What did you feel when you saw the stained glass window?" I ask Mark.

"I can almost not describe it," he says. "Seeing our name in that synagogue was thrilling. It gave me a very moving sense of my own history."

In the small Montgomery park where Mark walks his dogs, Baptist church "captains" run around proselytizing, asking if you are Christian and, if so, have you been "saved," and, finally, if you are not a Baptist. If you aren't Christian or don't believe in God, they'll press a red sticker onto your lapel, meaning that you are on your way to hell. If you are Christian but not saved or a Baptist, then you get a yellow sticker, meaning you might be saved from the lake of fire if you eventually see the light; and if you are both saved and a Baptist, then you get a green sticker, meaning that the path to heaven is wide open for you, heaven being severely "restricted," like country clubs, golf courses, and professorships used to be.

Because Mark is a spokesman for the Southern Poverty Law Center, he and his family are targeted by the white supremacist hate groups whose activities the center monitors. Their house is surrounded by television cameras, their images constantly on view by security people at the center. A police car is always parked near his house, sometimes with a cop inside, sometimes not, but hopefully threatening enough to keep the bad boys away. My son and his family are mostly unruffled (for how else could they live?) but, even though I'm enormously proud of the work he and the center are engaged in, I fear for their lives. In many ways, being in the present American South is like being in present-day Poland. Hatreds seethe in both populations, sometimes expressed, sometimes in abeyance. My body becomes more rigid, more fearful, seemingly always on guard for signs of injustice.

Well known and justifiably celebrated for his even-handed reporting of hate incidents that sprout up all over the country, so far Mark has been tolerated by the danger-ous, gun-toting people who inhabit white supremacist mili-tias, and by venomous interviewers on Fox News and other Tea Party crackpots. His bravery, clear-mindedness, and fine writing skills; his powers of concentration and long, hard, daily hours of work bring me great pleasure and enor-mous pride.

Unlike me, an emotional ranter by nature, my son pre-fers judgment based on scholarship, the seriousness dis-played in academic historical studies. Even though I agree that a well-written scholarly work has its special seductive-ness and charm, a look back into history, not to speak of ongoing events, is based largely on personal interpretation and is thus trustworthy only up to a point. I respect my son's love of "serious" tomes, but I wish he trusted fiction as a way of truth telling as much as he trusts nonfiction.

In Warsaw he was invited to visit the then-nearly-completed Museum of Jewish History whose construction had not given me great hope for the re-education of an anti-Semitic public, whereas Mark was capable of seeing it as a promising step forward. "I like your ability to not pre-judge it," I tell him. "I wish I could think of it as positively as you do."

Then Mark tells me that while he and Carol sat in an outdoor café in the great Market Square of Krakow, they witnessed a huge demonstration organized by a very popular reactionary radio station, with thousands of marchers high-stepping and singing patriotic songs, holding up red and white Polish flags and signs proclaiming that Poland is for the Poles only.

Mark and Sarah's mother, from whom they inherited half their genes, was an Episcopalian from Tulsa, Oklahoma and, in spite of my children's being born in Paris and Mallorca, they are both American in a way that I am not, and thus much more distant from the history that I carry around with me, including not only the traumas but the sense of not belonging.

When Sarah flies East for a visit, we harness our dogs and head into town, Gabriel stopping as always for a sniff at his usual pee stops, Sarah and Zelda going on ahead. We get off the cement path leading away from the State House and sit down on the grass, wonderful flower smells all around us. "My memories of sitting at a long table at the Plainfield Grange for our political Seders are lovely," Sarah tells me when I steer the conversation to our mutual sense of belonging. "They were full of family and friends, a sweet part of my history." We lie down next to each other, my beautiful daughter's head on my shoulder. "My memories of sitting at a long table in Greece or Italy with Mama and Peter, on the boat or wherever," she says after a few moments of silence, "were very different. I belonged there only by the skin of my teeth, battling for recognition. With everyone at the table dead drunk, I'd fall asleep in my chair. It was awful." She settles Zelda, who is sniffing the fragrant grass. "I love being part of a warm, inclusive, judgmental, argumentative tribe. Even though those Plainfield Seders were pretty outrageous, even comical in retrospect with their political correctness and liberation theology, they did follow a Haggadah especially re-written for lefty occasions such as ours."

"I am a Jew," Sarah says, surprising me a little with the vehemence of her statement. "I love the Jewish world with its warmth and joy in discussing everything, never taking anything for granted. I love that. As for the property in Krakow," she says, "I have zero feelings about it. All I know is your lifelong attitude about Poland."

Even when she was quite little, my beautiful daughter stumbled in a dark room, knocking over blocks she had put together during the day. The first time Joan made me aware of Sarah's apparent night blindness, a terrible dread filled my body, perhaps my first feeling about the inevitability of something loosely defined as destiny. The worst of it was thinking that this little beauty, a little "Brigitte Bardot," according to my father, would go blind.

Upon graduating from college, Mark's first job was as labor reporter for the *Hammond Times* of Indiana. On one of his visits home, I took him to a small party of artists and art supporters. He could not contain his disdain the next morning at breakfast, telling me that he would have preferred a father who was a labor organizer rather than an artist—a poignant memory that now makes me smile, remembering that wonderful young man, smitten by his growing importance in the journalism world. It hurt at the time. As for my daughter, surely she would have preferred a father who did not pass his blindness on to her.

Just as Mark would have preferred Saul Alinsky as a father, Sarah deserved a father free of this dread gene and, being stuck with it, one who did not suck up all the attention at a time when teenage Sarah needed all the attention she could get, as well as a strong and resolute father. Not only was she living with my emotional absence, more accurately a sporadic presence, she was devastated by her mother's abandonment and neglect in Greece, which created an unfillable well.

None of us knew much about happy families. Joan and

I came from families that each of us felt compelled to flee and, having done so, we played out whatever seductive examples came to our juvenile, adventurous minds, living, we thought, like D. H. and Frieda Lawrence, Gerald and Sara Murphy and the Lost Generation admirers they attracted. Joan, also an only child, did everything she could to get away from her Oklahoma mother and father, to the extent of marrying a Jewish refugee artist, about as far from her origins as possible; while Charlotte, who came into my life later, ran from her own dysfunctional family, which included a despised mother, a glorified father, and four brothers: the slumlord Irwin who, filthy rich, spent time in prison; a brother who was poisoned while in the Navy during World War II and presumed dead; another who was a docile part-time archivist; and Jerry, who spent his entire life in Israel, a righteous life-long kibbutznik, the only one she truly loved. Still, Charlotte and I tried hard to coalesce around our kids, house, and friends and, if nothing else, succeeded in creating the look of stability.

When Sarah reminds me of our times at the Museum of Modern Art or watching Mamet's *A Life in the Theater* in the Village or sitting next to each other at another performance of *The Nutcracker*, I beam, thrilled to recall instances of sharing so many things when they were young.

"Papa, you were a huge force in my life," Sarah says. "You were very loving when you wanted to be. You sat with me for hours on those brightly colored couches in the living room, listening to Mozart. I always knew that you loved me. You let me sit on your lap and lean my ear into your neck and listen to your after-dinner coffee go down your throat. You let me fluff up your hair and make you look like a clown." We move into the kitchen where Sarah makes us tea. Even though she chides herself for having been clunky, in fact she moves with enormous grace. "You were present and loving when you were there. Charlotte became more jealous of your time, and you were more involved in either going blind or your friends. Mark and I used to joke, 'Here comes another best friend into Papa's life.' "

"The best friends were as essential as sunlight, and the oncoming blindness consumed all my attention."

Our house was a welcoming haven. In the course of nearly thirty years, nothing gave me more pleasure than bringing gifts for the house or fixing its endless list of deteriorating parts, some as fundamental as foundation walls, some ornamental, like the almost-Tiffany chandelier saved from the wreckage of a colonial revival house on Boston's Beacon Hill, which then cast its warm yellow-orange light on the dining table. My old Vermont farmhouse grew more beautiful and welcoming every year. The kitchen was a blend of rosy cherrywood cabinets, pounded iron hinges and knobs, tiled counters, a butcher-block peninsula under green-shaded hanging lights.

At Thanksgiving dinner on Richardson Street, Mark says, "Remember when you took me to that opera? We went to a restaurant before, the time you introduced me to calves' brains. Can't find them so easily anymore," my son says, then remembers the opera we saw, *The Love for Three Oranges*. And that movie, one of the first made by a black director, Melvin Van Peebles's *Sweet Sweetback's Baadasssss Song*."

Looking back at moments with Mark and Sarah brings me great joy and comfort. It reassures me that, however flawed my fathering was, my children and I shared many memorable times, and that being a decent father does not require learning by example. All in all, the Potok survivors, a few in Australia, one in Sweden, my dearest cousin and her family in London, Mark, Sarah, and I, aren't doing too badly. As a matter of fact, we are privileged in countless ways.

Mark and Sarah's children—Anna, Rachel, and Nickie—

have no contact with my old world, its story a foggy irrelevance. On the other hand, I can imagine a future descendant, maybe even with a different surname, who might be attracted by any of the family's twentieth- and twenty-first-century dramas. One day, one of them might receive a call from Artur's son in Krakow that the recovery and sale of the Stradomska Street property has been accomplished and a large sum of money will be routed to their bank accounts.

11

REPARATIONS

1.

Three short e-mails arrive from Edward Prokocimer's son in Israel, Miron Prokocimer, who wrongly
inherited the Stradomska Street property. The first sounds
mildly uninterested:

"I have received a mail from my cousin P. Prokocimer
regarding the property located in Stradom 13 Krakow," he
writes. "Many years ago I have approached the issue on
behalf of my late mother. Many of the facts which Mr.
Borowsky [who is he?] has mentioned in his letter were not
known to me. I have stopped dealing with this issue years
ago. I am not interested in the matter in any way, and I do
not want any part in this claim. I will be more than glad to
meet you in the future, and regain contact with the remaining Prokocimer family members."

The next e-mail states that he expects an immediate
answer from me, writing that he thinks it important that
he and I have direct contact concerning this matter. "Nota-
bly I have a different information regarding the tragic death
of Paulina Prokocimer-Potok H"YD during the Holocaust," he writes. "I am really looking forward to hear from

you. Please answer. As stated yesterday you do not have any conflict of interests with me regarding the building in Krakow. The same is true with Phillipe Prokocimer and his siblings."

Another note arrives, in a surprisingly friendly tone. He writes: "Hello Andrew, It is really exciting to have found you! We are true cousins of second degree!" He attaches a photograph. "Is the man on the right side of the photo your father?" he asks. It was not. "The lady on the left and the gentleman next to her are my late parents: Helena and Dr. Edward Prokocimer. The picture must have been taken sometime in the early thirties. Shabbat shalom, Miron."

I forward the Miron correspondence to Artur and Basia, who then write the following to Miron Prokocimer:

> "I am contacting you on behalf of Mr. Artur Bobrowski and Mr. Marcin Kosiorkiewicz—who represent your cousin—Mr. Andrew Potok. As you already know, there are pending proceedings in Krakow Court with regard to Paulina Prokocimer and her siblings' inheritance (one half of a tenement located in Krakow), and more specifically—regarding to the change of the old court's decision. The actual title book appoints only you and your mother, which is/was an effect of a mistake from 1940s. As result of the actual proceedings, the ownership will be newly split as follows:
>
> • one-fourth for Andrew Potok,
> • one-eighth for you and your mother,
> •one-eighth for Bruno Prokocimer's children.
>
> "All parties—as natural heirs—are involved and must participate. Having said that, we kindly ask you to provide contact details to your attorney in Poland, and in case you don't have any, your physical address for

receipt of court's correspondence. Thank you very much upfront.

"Our client mentioned, you are not interested in this matter, which seems kind of incomprehensible, since there is no conflict between the parties, but only a mistakenly disclosed ownership title (to you and your mother). Thank you."

Basia then writes me with the numbers:

"Further to our yesterday's e-mail, we wanted you to know that the property should generate an income of approximately ~10–15,000 USD (brutto)/per month. Keeping it simple, it is about ~100,000 USD /per year (after taxes & other costs). According to the Polish law, the building's administrator is obligated (if required) to present all settlements of accounts for the past 10 years, and repay old incomes. Assuming that the property generated about ~500,000 USD in the last five years and additional ~ 250,000 USD in the previous five years (2003–2008), Artur thinks that you and your cousins theoretically should be paid ~300–400,000 USD. We want you to know, Andrew, that Miron (Marian) Proko-cimer is appointed in the Land Register Book of the tenement. If he responds to your e-mail, please ask him kindly, if he has ever received any profits out of the property rents, and if not, if any administrator has ever presented him reports concerning monthly or yearly income. We want him to know and realize, that you are aware of all these information."

I am thoroughly confused. It's the first time I hear that Miron is expected to return the inflated proceeds from the property or that I am to expect an annual income rather than the money from a sale of the recovered property. And then, could they really be expecting Miron to simply mail a check or willingly show up in a Polish court? Artur and Basia do not threaten with a lawsuit, and Miron, undoubtedly feeling safe from prosecution, seems not to care one way or another.

For the moment, the entire process is being slowed by my newfound second cousin Philippe's request that everything be translated into French and sent to his siblings in Paris. And as Artur's Krakow office is about to close for the summer, Basia forwards a note from the archives of Statens Utlänningskommission (State Aliens Commission), the Swedish National Archive. "The Potok family got a visa for travelling through Sweden for the period 30 September to 16 October 1939," it reads. "They arrived in Sweden on 6 October 1939. They applied for prolongations of the visas, which were granted for the periods 17 October to 16 December 1939, and 17 December 1939 to 25 January 1940."

I read this over and over again, having so little documentation about the four-month journey from Warsaw, through Lithuania and Latvia, then to Sweden, and from Bergen in Norway to New York. Our crossing into Lithuania occurred on probably the last day before the Soviets occupied that country. The Lithuanian border must have closed around the seventeenth of September. The dates given by the Swedish Archives are puzzling because I remember nothing between Lithuania and Stockholm, not until Anita informs me that we stayed a week in Riga. I had assumed that Latvia fell to the Soviets about the same time as Lithuania, which would have made a week's stay in Riga impossible, but this turned out not to be true. Latvia was not occupied by Russians until 1940, and by Germans in 1942, after which the killing of Jews inside Latvia was monumental.

Anita's story of her mother's arranging for an airplane

to fly us from Riga to Sweden had never been a part of my exodus story before, but neither had many other moments, none of which will ever be substantiated, there being no survivors left who can speak the truth about our history. Even when our parents were alive, their stories were suspect, often self-serving. As far as any knowledge of our murdered family was concerned, they either didn't know or the horror back there was better left without comment. Why even discuss it? In any case, truth was always trumped by expediency, the need to please, to mollify, to heal, even though attention was always paid to words spoken by the powerful, the celebrities, the wealthy patron, the doctor, anyone in a position of authority.

Recently, Anita also claimed to have seen not only her father's passport but a car registration that identified our van not as a Citroen but a Chevrolet. I am amazed. Our Polish diminutive for the Citroen automobile, Citronka, still reverberates in my ears, not only from my childhood but from its being referred to by my mother over many years.

I have often dreamed about finding a receipt of gasoline bought on the road to Lithuania, the registration of the sky blue Packard, the airplane ticket from Latvia to Stockholm, a note from the school Anita and I attended there, the steamship ticket from Norway on the Bergensfjord, a photo of us arriving at Ellis Island. But even if photographs did exist, they would no longer be available to me, one of the little-noted losses of blindness. Missing from my life are photographs of my children as they were growing up, whatever photos exist of my family, alive and dead, of my beautiful Loie, of landscapes I once loved, photographs of any of us in Paris, Barcelona, Palma de Mallorca, Florence and Venice and Rome, Mytilini and Molyvos and Athens, the Saski Gardens in Warsaw.

2.

Still our woodpecker has not appeared. I sit on our porch listening to the blue jays and chickadees as I sniff the wild roses and black snake weed in front. I'm thinking of the "Polish shit" which has had such a profound effect on my life, both covering me in a carapace of hate and opening me to deeper reflection and retrospection, to a better understanding of human obsessions, the spectrum of emotional and intellectual striving, the power of imagination, the rage for the control necessary to sit in judgment of injustice, despair, war and peace.

When in a mellower mood, I try to imagine kinder ways to look at the perfidious Edward Prokocimer and his son Miron, born a year after his father's testimony, whose casual dismissal of the attempt to correct the wrongful inheritance of Number Thirteen Stradomska seems to be working to his advantage. Now in his sixties, Miron most likely can't accept, or even imagine, his father's likely guilt.

Three years have passed since our Krakow excursion and, answering my questions about its progress, specifically about Miron's participation, Artur writes that the Polish court is still waiting for proof of the death of three members of my murdered family. "The probate case in Krakow is suspended until that proceeding is closed," he writes. "For now, no attorney representing Miron or his cousins has joined the proceeding. But this is not a problem because we have their addresses and the court will notify them of the proceedings by post." All of this once seemed more urgent, more imminent. "The only problem is that this will take more time," Artur writes. I'll say.

"Best to forget about it," Loie says. "But it's not a dead end," she adds. "Not yet anyway."

"That woodpecker was all fucked up."

"He should have been pecking at a 'Beware of Falling Rocks' or 'Rogue Waves' sign," Loie says.

There seems to be no way of hurrying my case but, eager to know how it is proceeding, I again ask Basia who writes:

> "We are not being in touch with the Prokocimer family because your case is totally independent. Miron and others are not holding up your proceeding, it simply takes so much time. It is hard to estimate how long will it take, but we are currently going through a necessary proceeding re declaring of your cousin—Ludwik Sereth and his father, Izydor—officially dead. Ludwik was Izydor Sereth and Maryla vel Maria Potok's son. Maria vel Maryla was your father's sister. Back in 1946, when Edward Prokocimer was declaring everybody dead, he "forgot" about Izydor and his son. According to the court's understanding/law, when somebody is not dead (death certificate)—he or she is still alive. Such proceedings take about six or seven months at least, from announcement, that needs to be published for minimum six months, until official court's decision and issuing of a new death certificate. After it is done (Ludwik and Izydor are declared officially dead), we will be able to move forward with the actual claim/proceeding."

Easy does it, Potok. These people, the close relatives I knew nothing about, were murdered seventy-five years ago. With the exception of Maryla's son who might have survived all these years as I did, the law requires death certificates of people who, if still alive, would be more than a hundred years old. Still, I learn that Maryla was married to a man named Izydor Sereth and had a son named Ludwik, to be added to the long list of strange names that preceded mine, Andrew being as distant from Wladyslaw or Zbyg-niew as humanly possible, my parents' way of assuring themselves that their son would be prepared for inevitable flight.

3.

Though I'm imprisoned in my history, I am scratch-ing my way out. In yogaland, I rock my pelvis, circle my knees, stretch into the pigeon, the frog, the downward fac-ing dog. I concentrate on my breathing without help from higher powers, without sending energy into the ether. I do it in part to be physically flexible but also to rid myself of the outside world. "Breathe, breathe, put all your awareness on your breath," Robert the yoga master says. He directs yoga sessions in his "yoga hut." When I confide my various psychic pains, Robert often says, "It's moment by moment" or "day by day." I try to find the wisdom in this and suspect that I'm not looking deeply enough. "Breathe into it," Rob-ert says, words that might be the ultimate wisdom, as much as one person can say to help another. I love this man's mind for its encyclopedic knowledge of baseball. He might repeat himself giving psychological advice, but he can make the 1951 World Series come alive, the who, the where, the how, plus the numbers. Robert has an altar enshrining a smiling, androgenous Buddha, a photograph of the Dalai Lama, and one of Mickey Mantle. The numbers 21 and 42, once on the back of Paul O'Neill's and Mariano Rivera's uniform, are numbers Robert celebrates. What's not to like?

But my moods vacillate wildly. At certain moments, I look back on the events in my life and their probable causes as extraordinary, stories worthy of careful mining; I scratch for themes, then give them order and shape, my life as parabola or pyramid, a one-way street with no exits, no U-turns allowed. Moments later, I'm aware only of a pile of unresolved chaos, small pleasures and pains, one damned thing after another. Post-Krakow, the awakening of dormant issues in my mind stoking a burgeoning anger, I miss the role painting once had in my life, transporting me from the harsh realities outside my skin into momentary playfulness, away from the world of objects, the world of power and lies and anecdotes, back to the purity of hand and body movements, back to the fresh stirrings of the imagination, back to work that is the consequence of a profound, relentless, unquenchable need for an experience that is by nature intense, immediate, vivid, another mode of thought.

I think daily of painting again, this time with no vision at all. In my mind's eye, very large surfaces are thick with ochres and lemon yellows, textured with sandy particles and enriched by dripping cadmium reds, all threatened by walls of impastoed black. My body trembles with emotion. I return to normal breathing, the territory behind my eyelids back to its irritating sickly greenish yellow, the color of blindness. Next time I conjure up a painting, it is full of faces and bodies, mute or shrieking, still or wriggling, crowded humanity. An artist friend wants to help me put whichever of the images I choose onto canvas but, as we begin to make preparations in the attic of my house or an extra room in hers, I find excuses, frightened by the craziness of the venture, the nightmarish frustration that is sure to accompany the act.

The entire painting process for people like me is outside the parameters of "normal," and any departure from normal—painting while demented, schizophrenic, bipolar, drunk, high on drugs, or blind—puts one in a special category, with an asterisk beside the name, like the baseball player who breaks the record on steroids or during a longer season. Given all the abnormal states of mind or body, it's difficult to determine if the work is based on deep visions and convictions—made in creative struggle, an art that takes us to another level of knowing and understanding— or if it's gibberish, meaningless, contrived.

On the other hand, much exquisite work in every art is the product of one "abnormality" or another. Some artists pine for pain and suffering, making it up if it doesn't exist, feeling in their guts that it's a prerequisite for inspired work. The great American poet John Berryman wrote, "I do strongly feel that among the greatest pieces of luck for high achievement is ordeal. Certain great artists can make out without it, Titian and others, but mostly you need ordeal. My idea is this. The artist is extremely lucky to be presented with the worst possible ordeal which would not actually kill him . . . Beethoven's deafness, Goya's deafness, Milton's blindness, that kind of thing. And I think that what happens with my poetry work in the future will largely depend not on my sitting on my ass as I think mmm, a long poem again? but on being knocked in the face and thrown flat and given cancer and all kinds of other things. Short of senile dementia . . . I hope to be nearly crucified." Berryman's severe depression did not lead to greater poetry but to suicide.

Most artists and writers stop trying by their eighties at the latest, but when one knows that there is little time left, the late work produced can be a generous emptying of an old or disabled man's mind, offered with abandon, representing the man in all the stages of his life. Of course, not all such work is a calm emptying out. Often, it is irascible, uncaring, immensely demanding. Edward Said, a great music critic, wrote: "The accepted notion is that age confers a spirit of reconciliation and serenity on late works, often expressed in terms of a miraculous transfiguration of reality . . . but each of us can supply evidence of late works which crown a lifetime of aesthetic endeavor. Rembrandt and Matisse, Bach and Wagner. But what of artistic lateness not as harmony and resolution, but as intransigence, difficulty and contradiction? What if age and ill health don't produce serenity at all?" How has the Krakow experience influenced not only my writing but the possible images that might still emerge from this old but eager mind and body? At the age of seventy-six, Samuel Becket said, "With diminished concentration, loss of memory, obscured intelligence, the more chance there is for saying something closest to what one really is."

4.

My Polish rant has given me—and this is a word so hackneyed that I have a hard time using it—the journey, the existential journey. As the Alexandrian Greek poet Constantine Cavafy wrote over a hundred years ago:

> When you set sail for Ithaca,
> wish for the road to be long,
> full of adventures, full of knowledge . . .
> Ithaca gave you the marvelous journey.
> Without her you would not have set out.
> She has nothing left to give you now.

When I began this book, its trajectory seemed clear. It would record my facing the old devils once again, the righting of wrongs and the collecting of rewards by way of a deus ex machina, a satisfying resolution. Improbable things do happen. Some people do survive in spite of great odds against it. We got out of Poland, not a gift of God but a sequence of, say, twenty random, often lucky, events—not nineteen but twenty.

But though Cavafy's journey to Ithaca has become a tired concept, it is nevertheless true that the lessons inherent in the pursuit itself represent the real treasure. The recovery and sale of the Thirteen Stradomska Street property might happen one day but probably not in my lifetime.

Whether it is the fault of the Polish legal system or the ineptitude of Artur and his colleagues I do not know. Even if the property were somehow wrested from Miron's hands, given the fact of its decrepitude, its sale for more than a token amount of *zlotys* seems improbable.

As unsatisfying as the lack of a magical denouement might be, the pain and pleasure experienced through the writing of this book has been the primary reward. I have not emerged victorious, but enriched. The process began with my dramatic performance at the Warsaw Airport, the breakdown unleashing a year of awareness, a release of old baggage and openness to the new. Waiting at the Frederic Chopin Airport in an unmoving line, the regular working security crew on strike and replaced by non-professionals, a connecting flight about to leave without us and, above all, not seeing. I was stranded inside echoing stone walls, surrounded by a whispering, grumbling crowd. I was ignorant, invisible, having no say, no control over a seemingly life-changing situation. I was living the helplessness of a terrorized eight-year-old facing the unknown, the end of life as he knew it, his only reality nothingness, sitting terrorized in the Citroen van, the helpless child, seeing only blackness and extinction, all of life in the hands of others: the man who showed up to furnish gasoline for the van's empty gas tank, the hateful farmer's wife who boiled two chickens for an Apfelbaum mink coat, the snarling soldiers at border crossings, replaced now in the same Polish language by the scabs who controlled our passage.

Until this third trip to Poland, I had transformed the bombs and bullets, the improbability of our escape, into war stories, an adventure. It came easily, evoking not pity but wonder. It was Andy's golden childhood, innocent Andy bombed in the middle of an unkempt field, brave Andy making a new life for himself. The movie, the hermetic story, then exploded into shards of pain, depression, and anger. I was forced to face reality from a new perspective, reading new histories of the war, memoirs of the Holocaust, books about anti-Semitism and Judaism. I forgot how to smile, even how to love. But better understanding a life lived does not necessarily lead to euphoria or resolution. There is no closure, no expectation of justice. There can be no moving on, no forgiveness, no clarity, no abatement of rage. My blood still boils but more often these days it merely simmers, still unable to tolerate perpetrators, bystanders, nations acting like nations, anyone whose life is influenced by babble from holy books or television serials, anyone who truly believes that their God doles out only what humans can handle. On each of my visits several Poles have recommended forgetting and reconciliation. *"Pan Andrzej,* you must let bygones be bygones. That was then; this is now." But what was then has not disappeared and I doubt that I will ever find a way to forgive priests and bishops, mullahs and imams, the establishment, for hating my kind. After the damage that faith has caused in the world, the concept of faith remains a danger, the lurking cloud that doesn't go away, forever threatening the planet.

Delving deeper into any aspect of human behavior does not fill me with hope. On the contrary, it is frightening. It does not get better. A surfeit of hatred does not prevent future hatred. The more I know, the more hopeless the plight of this planet and its inhabitants becomes. Human morality has not improved and everything I experience, everything I learn anew, hammers that truth home. Perhaps Poland really is no worse than anywhere else on the planet. Perhaps the immorality of our species is dictated by natural selection and we can't escape it.

If one doesn't learn to move on, to let go, to let bygones be bygones, then what? Syria, Afghanistan, Iraq, almost everywhere in post-colonial Africa, as well as Mexico and Central America, have forced the world to rethink its purported humanity, and the response has been predictably inhuman. Poland has voted in a far right government—bigoted, Catholic in its most medieval, primitive sense, utterly reactionary—whose aim is to assert its hateful Polish Catholicism by rejecting the immigration of Muslims. According to my Swedish cousin Anna, even Jews are seen as preferable to those new others. In building the Jewish historical museum, the Poles knew they could safely honor the part that Jews once played in the life of the country, knowing that they are not about to witness a new influx of Jews. Of course it's not just Poland but the once admired democracies of Europe that now feel threatened by another loathsome religion. Here in the United States, half the country would like to send the dirty, leprous Latin Americans back to be murdered in the countries of their origins, made unlivable by American corporate and military thugs and death squads.

On the one hand, we have greed and the yearning for power; on the other we have the Bach *Musical Offering* and *The Art of Fugue*, Homer's *Odyssey*, Shakespeare's *King Lear*, the Velazquez *Las Meninas*. When I sit in my comfortable living room and listen to a late Beethoven quartet or piano sonata, to Mahler's *Das Lied von der Erde*, all the pain and hatred leave me. I am immersed in the truth of art. I know that the species I am part of has attained these extraordinary transcendent levels of being. They fill me with wonder and deep satisfaction.

5.

As a stiff early winter wind shakes the bedroom windows in the middle of a sleepless night, I again conjure up my grandparents.

"When you saw it coming, did you turn toward god or

did you already know that god was dead and that nothing could save you?" I ask.

"*Jendrush*, dear *Jendrush*," Paulina says, using my little boy diminutive, "this is a complicated question. We were not sure. We wanted to believe in something but it became more and more difficult. Mostly we were—how do they say it, *Solek*?—yes, agnostic. And I think all our children came to the same conclusion."

I tell them that piety and anti-Semitism still thrive. "Even back in Vermont where some of the strangest beliefs are tolerated, you better watch out before you tell anyone you're an atheist."

"We were agnostics but word of this did not pass through the front door," my grandfather Solomon says.

I am relieved. This is my family. "There is so much I want to know. What did you think about Freud, Marx, Tolstoy, Shakespeare, Moliere, Mickiewicz? Did you have a favorite painting, a Rembrandt or a Titian? Did you love Schubert or Viennese waltzes? Surely Chopin."

"He read Tolstoy and Chekhov in Russian," my grandmother says, nudging her husband. "I loved those French painters—you know—those boating parties, the girls who kicked their legs so high, the flowers."

"If only the world turned out the way you wanted," I tell them, almost in tears, "you would have finished your lives so differently, possibly with a quiet death at home, surrounded by your children and by me, we who love you."

"It does sometimes happen like that," my grandmother says.

A poem I love pops into my head and I get out of bed, go to my computer to get it right. I find the document, Wyslawa Szymborska's "On Death, Without Exaggeration," and my computer reads it aloud.

It can't take a joke,
find a star, make a bridge.
It knows nothing about weaving, mining,
farming,
building ships, or baking cakes . . .
Sometimes it isn't strong enough
to swat a fly from the air.
Many are the caterpillars
that have outcrawled it . . .

6.

At the end of this summery day in October, I feel safe and content. Loie and I have made a succulent braised pot roast for dinner. Tomorrow a first-class chamber music concert awaits us in town and the World Series is about to begin.

In the middle of the night, I wake from a dream in which I am trying to find my way home in a rural landscape. Even though my eyesight is intact, it's getting late and I want to get home before nightfall. Some paths are familiar; most are not. Every once in a while, I come upon a house, knock on a door, and ask directions. Each time, a man steps out of his house to point the way, nodding toward a small path or no path at all, and always a steeper climb. Each man is kind, encouraging, eager to help. New hills appear every time I think I have come to the end, which somehow doesn't dissuade me from going on. Finally, I hear Loie's voice in the distance. "You're almost home," she says.

ACKNOWLEDGMENTS

My return to Poland, the basis for this book, would not have been possible without the extraordinary help of my wife, Loie Morse, who suffered the indignities of March weather in Krakow with me and helped me navigate the memories of my early life that emerged during that visit. Loie kept me sane and safe not only in Poland but also at home in Vermont during the nearly three years it took to write this book.

With his intelligence, compassion, and generosity, my friend Mathew Rubin helped me manage the volatile emotions that this writing provoked. And then there is Richard Witte whose hours of listening to my book-related kvetches and responding with friendship and intelligence also made a huge difference in whatever quality this book achieves.

This book has gone through several transformations of structure and content, reflecting my slowly evolving interpretation of history, both personal and political. I am grateful to Chris Lynch and Sally Brady for their early editing help, but most of all I thank Mary Beth Hinton for her masterful editing of the emergent final version. The generous reading and suggestions offered by Jay Neugeboren, Elinor Langer, and Lawrence Weschler greatly benefited this book.

Without the technical assistance of the Vermont Division for the Blind and especially the patience and love of Geoff and Peggy Howard, I don't believe that I could have managed the difficulties that blindness imposes on the writing process. My stepson Jed Clifford was of great help when computer problems arose. Last, but assuredly not least, I thank The Seeing Eye, a magnificent resource for those of us within the blind population who choose to be guided by its beautifully trained guide dogs. The last two of the five dogs who have brought safety and love to my life—the now-retired noble Gabriel and the new black Lab wonder, Z—were both trained by the very best, Walt Sutton and Shannon Deuschle.

ABOUT THE AUTHOR

ANDREW POTOK was a successful visual artist until he lost his sight in his forties. Subsequently he authored several important books: *Ordinary Daylight: Portrait of An Artist Going Blind*, about his loss of eyesight and its impact on work, identity, and personal relationships; *My Life with Goya*, a novel about a young Jewish artist's life in America following World War II; *A Matter of Dignity: Changing the World of the Disabled*, portraits of therapists and activists who worked to more fully integrate disabled persons into mainstream American life; and *My Father's Keeper*, a novel about a father-son relationship marred by hatred and betrayal. He lives in Vermont.